ALETHEIA ADVENTU

The
DEFENDERS
OF ALETHEIA

E.M. WILKIE

THE DEFENDERS OF ALETHEIA

Aletheia Adventure Series Book 5

Book 2 of the Battle for Aletheia Trilogy

E M Wilkie

JOHN RITCHIE LTD
CHRISTIAN PUBLICATIONS

Copyright © 2015 by John Ritchie Ltd.
40 Beansburn, Kilmarnock, Scotland

www.ritchiechristianmedia.co.uk

ISBN-13: 978 1 910513 35 4

Written by E M Wilkie
Illustrated by E M Wilkie
www.aletheiabooks.co
Copyright © 2015

This is a work of fiction. The characters, incidents, and dialogues are products of the author's imagination and are not to be construed as real. Any resemblance to actual events or persons, living or dead, is entirely coincidental.

All rights reserved. No part of this book may be reproduced, distributed or transmitted in any form or by any means, including photocopying, recording, or other electronic or mechanical methods, without the prior written permission of the author, except in the case of non-commercial uses permitted by copyright law.

Cover illustration by Graeme Hewitson.
Interior illustrations are by E M Wilkie.

Unless otherwise indicated, Scripture quotations are taken from:
The Holy Bible, New King James Version®.
© 1982 by Thomas Nelson, Inc. Used by permission. All rights reserved.

To Zach, Bobby, Seth, Harry, Emily, Abigail and Olivia,
This story was written with the desire that you will all one day be Defenders of Bible Truth.

And to Benjamin,
for whom the Benjamin in this story is named.

"Being justified freely by His grace
through the redemption that is in Christ Jesus."
Romans 3:24

The Song of the Meddlers, from
The Mustardseeds, Aletheia Adventure Series Book 4:

"*They squabble and they do not pray*
The poison-blight will come [will come!]
The Meddlers' plan is here to stay
Aletheia will succumb [succumb! succumb! succumb!]
And now our cunning they will know
The city walls will fall [will fall!]
Aletheia is brought low, so low!
No drinkie-drink at all! [at all! no drinkie-drink at all!]"

PREFACE

This story is an attempt to help and encourage young readers to develop an understanding of the truth contained in the Word of God, the Bible. However, all characters, places, descriptions and incidents are entirely fictional and this adventure story is not intended to be a substitute for the teaching contained in the Bible, but rather an aid to understanding. The illustrations and allegories used in this story are not perfect; and therefore, whilst it is hoped that readers will benefit from the truth and lessons developed in this story, they must be urged to develop an understanding of Bible truth and doctrine from the Bible alone.

The author would like to acknowledge the invaluable help and advice of the following people who assisted in the production of this book:
M J Wilkie, R Hatt, A Henderson, R Chesney, and Margareta.
Many thanks to you all.

CONTENTS

Map of the City of Aletheia	9
Map of the Land of Err	10
Map of the Regions of Err	11
Prologue	13
Chapter 1: Underground Entry	18
Chapter 2: The Slide	26
Chapter 3: Underground Aletheia	36
Chapter 4: Above the Ground	46
Chapter 5: Management Meeting	52
Chapter 6: Josie's Idea	60
Chapter 7: Preparations for a Mission	66
Chapter 8: On a Mission!	73
Chapter 9: Dim View	82
Chapter 10: Enemy Territory	89
Chapter 11: Harold to the Rescue	98
Chapter 12: An Important Request	103
Chapter 13: Guard Duty	109
Chapter 14: Security Breach!	116
Chapter 15: Wonky Dollar	123
Chapter 16: The Debrief	132

Chapter 17: The Food Distribution Centre	138
Chapter 18: The Council of Err	147
Chapter 19: The Deceivedors	154
Chapter 20: Benjamin Escapes	164
Chapter 21: Mr Con Cozen	171
Chapter 22: Betrayed!	179
Chapter 23: Investigation	183
Chapter 24: Suspects	191
Chapter 25: Interview with Mr Mustardpot	195
Chapter 26: Catching the Spy	201
Chapter 27: Flight through Redemption Square	211
Chapter 28: Weighed in the Balances	221
Chapter 29: Strike Back	228
Chapter 30: All Go!	234
Chapter 31: The Battle for Aletheia	240
Chapter 32: The Outcome	251
Chapter 33: The Next Step	258
Chapter 34: Benjamin and the Judge	262
Chapter 35: The Last Defender of Aletheia	271
References	275

9

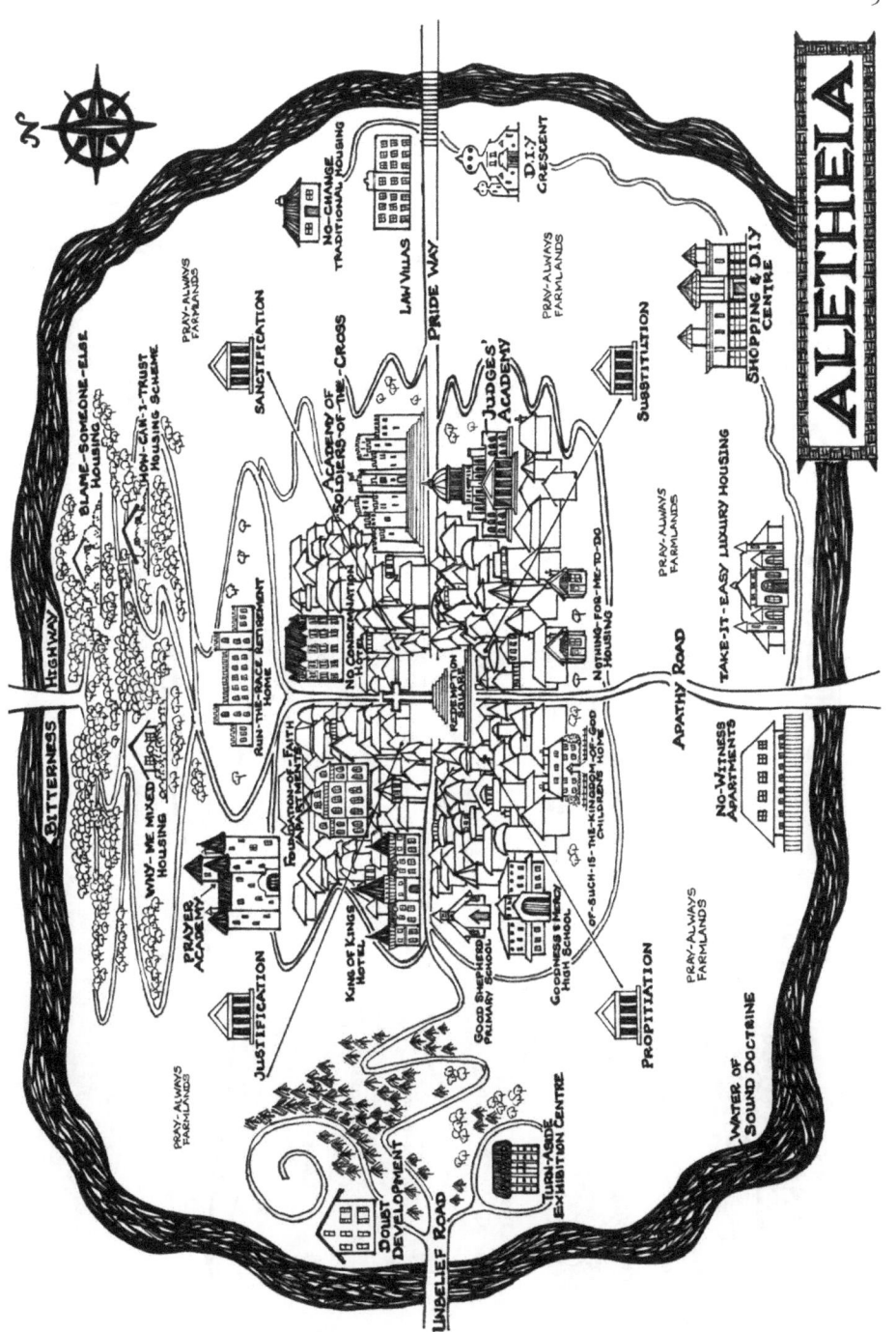

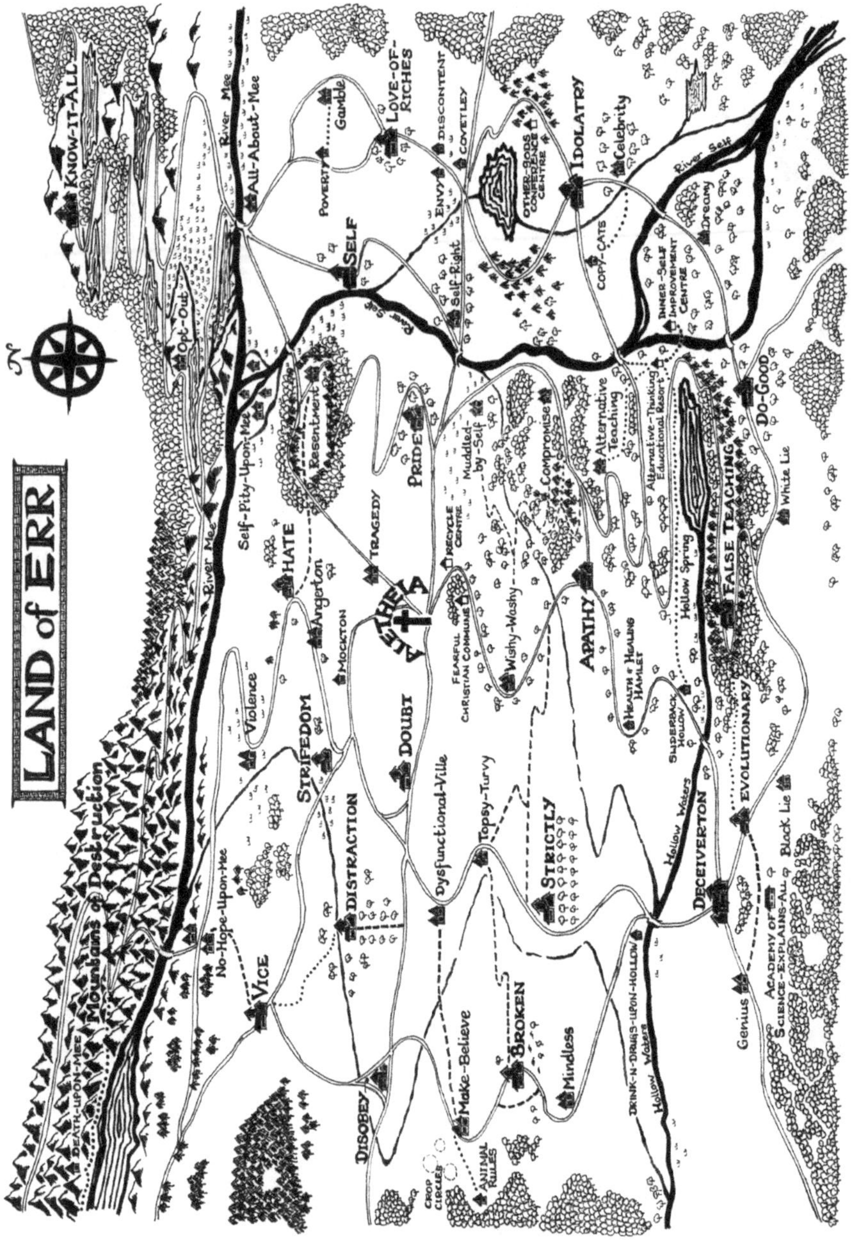
LAND of ERR
KNOW-IT-ALL
Mountains of Destruction
DEATH-UPON-MEE
River Mee
Opt-Out
All-About-Mee
Self-Pity-Upon-Mee
No-Hope-Upon-Mee
VICE
DISOBEY
Violence
STRIFEDOM
HATE
Angerton
MOCKTON
Resentment
SELF
POVERTY
Gamble
LOVE-OF-RICHES
DISCONTENT
ENVY
COVETLEY
OTHER-GODS CONFERENCE CENTRE
IDOLATRY
Celebrity
River Self
Self-Right
COPY-CATS
INNER-SELF IMPROVEMENT CENTRE
Dreamy
TRAGEDY
PRIDE
ALETHEIA
DOUBT
DISTRACTION
Dysfunctional-Ville
Make-Believe
BROKEN
Mindless
ANIMAL RULES
CROP CIRCLES
Topsy-Turvy
STRICTLY
FEARFUL CHRISTIAN COMMUNE
RECYCLE CENTRE
Muddled-by-Self
Wishy-Washy
Compromise
Alternative Teaching
Alternative-Thinking Educational Resort
APATHY
HEALTH & HEALING HAMLET
SLIDERBACK HOLLOW
Hollow Spring
Hollow Waters
FALSE TEACHING
DO-GOOD
White Lie
DECEIVERTON
EVOLUTIONARY
Black Lie
ACADEMY OF SCIENCE-EXPLAINS-ALL
Genius
DRINK-N-DRUGS-UPON-HOLLOW

11

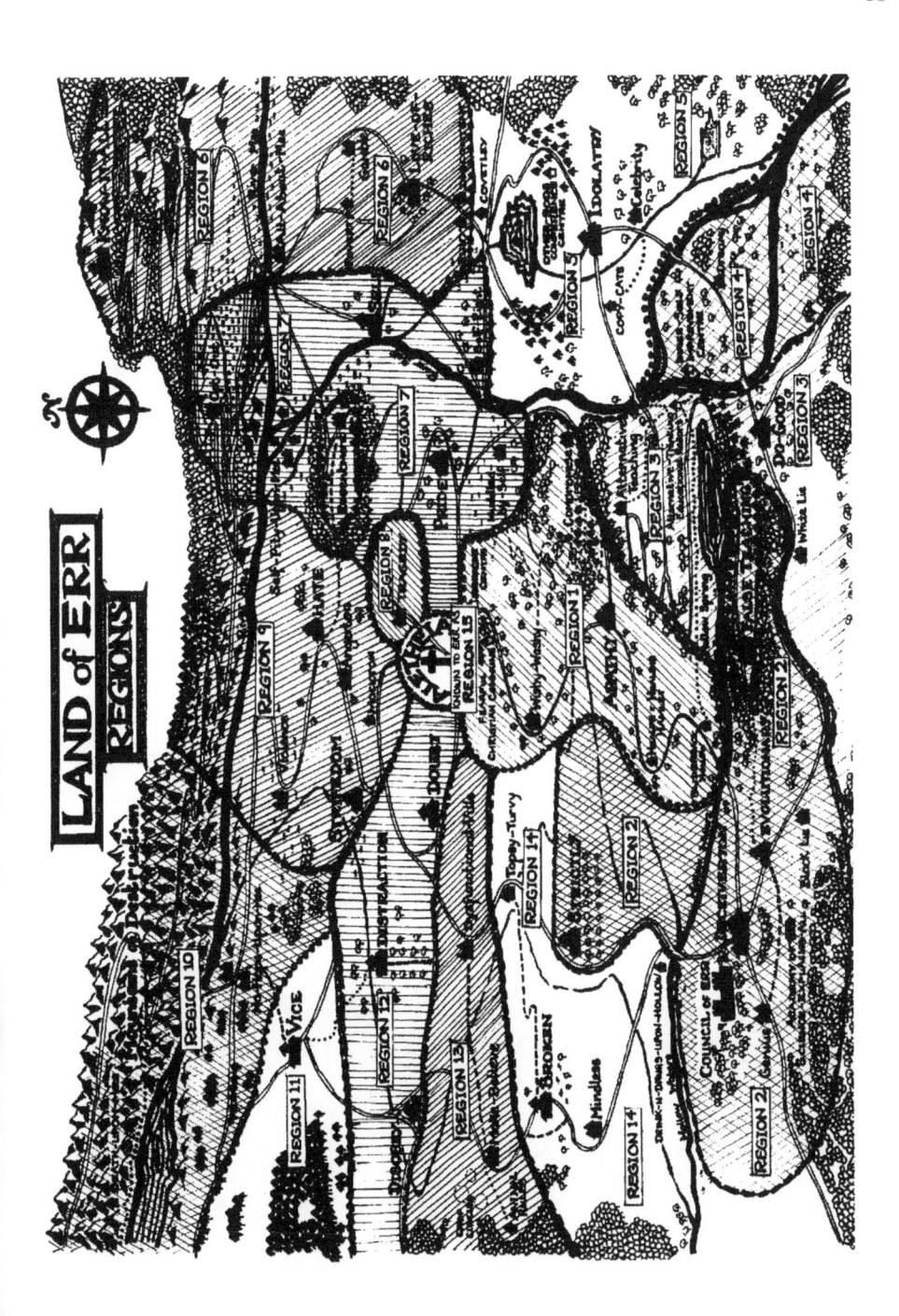

12 The Defenders of Aletheia

PROLOGUE

Rain lashed the streets of Aletheia and autumn leaves scurried into corners to huddle together in soggy heaps. Summer had long gone and this storm had the chill of winter about it. It was a sign of the times: the season of harvest and peace and plenty had passed for Aletheia, and a stormy blast was upon the city of Bible Truth.

Hugo Wallop stood stiff and attentive on guard duty within the confines of the building of Justification in the centre of the city. The rain could not get through the massive stone pillars at the front of the building, but it was easy to get cramped and cold standing on guard for another long shift.

Hugo stamped his feet and pressed both his hands around his Bible, feeling the warmth and comfort spilling from its pages. Between the pillars he could see through the slanting rain to the smouldering campfires of the invaders in Redemption Square. He was pleased to see they were all huddled uncomfortably in their makeshift tents and shelters, cramped and cold too. They had no pillars offering invisible protection, and no Bible to warm them either. The hordes who had overtaken the city wished to destroy the pillars of Justification and change it into something else. As for the Bible, the Word of God – in which the people of Aletheia placed all their confidence – their enemies from the land of Err wished to alter it entirely. And now they camped even in Redemption Square around the cross. Hugo had a fierce desire to see all the protesters washed clean out of the city by the drenching rain; to see them tumbling helter-skelter down one of the slopes that led out of Aletheia, over the Pray-Always Farmlands, and straight across the boundary, back to the land of Err from whence they came.

At least the storm meant that his shift was quiet. Usually he and Timmy Trial, his best friend and partner for guard duty, were contending with crowds of invaders from the land of Err, all curious about Aletheia. There were the officials and their workforce who had come to take over and transform the city; the tradesmen and tradeswomen who set up businesses to benefit from the changes in Aletheia; the teenagers and young people who came for the fun of it; the curious and the holiday-makers who camped on the Pray-Always Farmlands; and plenty of religious folk who were doing their best to take the message of Bible Truth the city stood for and change it into something more appealing to the land of Err. Already gold crosses and ornate churches were being constructed on The Outskirts of Aletheia. The new religion was nothing to do with the message of the Bible that trusting in the Lord Jesus was the only way people's sins could be forgiven[1]. Instead, people were offered forgiveness for money.

The Council of Err had quickly been successful in taking over The Outskirts, which were on the boundary of the city, furthest from the influence of the cross. It hadn't taken them long to invade the Pray-Always Farmlands either; they now resembled a huge, messy campsite. But the invaders of Err still could not gain access to the buildings in the centre of the ancient city. No matter how many times the officials from the land of Err tried to penetrate the open buildings, like Justification, or knock down the locked, Bible-access-only doors of the other buildings, they could not enter. When they touched the stones they received a most unpleasant sensation – a bit like an electric shock. When they peered in the windows, strange bright light blocked their view of anything within. They could not see the guard with Bible in hand; they could not see anything at all.

For reasons Hugo and Timmy did not understand, the building of Justification was particularly important in the defence of Aletheia. In these days of war, when every Christian, of all ages, was defending the city, it was an honour for them to guard the pillars of Justification;

it was a mark of the confidence of their commander, Hugo's cousin, Lieutenant Bourne Faithful, that they were granted such guard duty. Hugo stamped his feet again and heard Timmy's footsteps behind him. Timmy had just patrolled the building, walking through its stately corridors and polished courtroom, making doubly, triply certain all was safe and well.

"All quiet," he said cheerfully. He joined Hugo at the front pillars, looking out at the driving rain. "Hopefully the storm will keep them away today," he added.

Hugo nodded. The officials and builders and other workers had tried many times to enter through the pillars; they were not likely to want to get drenched trying again today. And the diggers and machinery they knew would one day be coming to attack them did not work without some sunlight to power them. The storm today felt like the protection of God. "I wonder why Justification is so important in this war," Hugo mused.

"It must be to do with the Truth here," said Timmy, having thought on this matter too. "There must be something here, in Justification, which will be important in defeating the lies of the new religions they're introducing."

"We'll explore it when we've got time," said Hugo.

Time was very hard to come by in these dangerous days. Every soul in Aletheia was constantly busy defending and praying and planning to overthrow their enemies and restore the city of Bible Truth.

For there was something the Council of Err did not know:

Aletheia might be polluted, besieged, and invaded – but they were not yet defeated.

CHAPTER 1
UNDERGROUND ENTRY

Summer was over and the fields were harvested and bare. The trees were beginning to change their leaves, dressing in the gold and orange shades of autumn. For Jack Merryweather, the end of the summer was a moment of great gloom. The previous summer he had gone to Aletheia on his very first adventure[2]. This summer, Aletheia was where he most wanted to be. But the holidays were past and with them, it seemed, had gone all hope of finding his way back to his friends in the faraway city of Aletheia. And Jack desperately needed to find his way back; he just didn't know how.

Aletheia was the name of the great city of Bible Truth situated in the centre of the mysterious land of Err. When Jack was last in Aletheia, the city was under threat. The troublesome Meddlers had hatched a plan to weaken the city[3]. They had tried to blight the Pray-Always Farmlands crops so that there would not be enough safe food for the people of Aletheia to eat in the year ahead. Thanks to Jack, and his friend, Hezekiah Wallop, the Meddlers hadn't succeeded. But the city was nonetheless weakened and confused, and was left clearing up a lot of horrid blight-goo left behind after the attempted attack. Jack hoped the harvest in Aletheia had been good. Was there enough safe food for the people of Aletheia?

Harris, Jack's younger brother, took the problems of Aletheia as seriously as Jack did. Harris loved hearing about Aletheia even though he'd never been there. He suggested stockpiling food from the kitchen in preparation for whenever they found their way to the city. He took a particular, and unusual, interest in 'Best Before' and 'Use By' labels on food jars and tins. He started storing them under his bed.

Of course, Jack knew that wasn't the solution to the problem. And besides, he knew there was something even more serious on the horizon for Aletheia – something worse than food-shortages. Jack and Hezekiah had discovered that the wicked Meddlers had another, more devious plan – hidden in a very silly song. Whilst the great city was still weakened, and its occupants were clearing up after the blight on the Pray-Always Farmlands, the Meddlers were planning an even more deadly attack. They were going to pollute the essential Water of Sound Doctrine. The people of Aletheia relied on the water to keep them right. It represented the whole, balanced Truth of the Bible. If the water was changed, the Bible Truth the city stood for was in danger. Had the Meddlers succeeded in destroying the water supplies and invading the city? What was happening to all his friends in Aletheia?

Jack sent several letters to his friend, Timmy Trial, who was from Jack's village of Steeple-Bumpton and was now in Aletheia. Timmy had special permission to be at school in Aletheia and he knew how to get there. But there was no word from Timmy. Perhaps the post had been stopped; perhaps it was a sign that the city had been besieged or invaded, or even destroyed!

Jack couldn't think of any other way of finding out what was happening in Aletheia. Harris, ever helpful, searched for news in the local newspapers. Harris couldn't read very well but he learned the word 'Aletheia' and diligently searched through items about weather, sport, lost cats, and local events, despite Jack's sceptical thoughts on the matter. Once Harris thought he had found something. But it was only a story about a woman called Althea which didn't have anything to do with Aletheia at all.

Jack's previous visits to Aletheia always began when he was least expecting it. So how did he *make* it happen? The only thing Jack knew about how Timmy went to Aletheia was that it was called 'Underground Entry'. And he had Timmy's address. That was all. And however many ways he tried to get underground, nothing worked. He dug a hole in the garden until Mum noticed and his plans came to an abrupt stop; he and Harris explored the caves by the beach on the family holiday; they even went on the London Underground. But there was no sign of entry into Aletheia. He prayed about it too, of course. Jack had learned from his adventures in Aletheia, in the land of Err, that prayer could do wonderful, powerful, unexpected things. But Jack also learned that the Bible taught that you must pray in the will of God, according to the teaching of the Bible[4]. And he wasn't clear where a trip back to Aletheia fitted in with that.

"What about Timmy's address?" Harris suggested one day, when they were both getting ready to go to school. "Maybe his address tells you how to get back to Aletheia."

Jack shook his head. He knew Timmy's address off by heart. It was slightly odd, but it didn't reveal much at all. It was 'PO Box 17, UGE, Direct Post, AL'.

"Perhaps it's to do with seventeen," said Harris hopefully.

"But seventeen *what?*" asked Jack gloomily.

Of course, Harris didn't know. But, all the same, it was Harris who spotted the significant telegraph pole. And it happened that very same day.

After school the two boys walked home. There was a bus stop with a small shelter at the side of the road, and, for reasons they could not have explained, both boys always ran in and out and around the bus shelter at least once on their way home. There was a telegraph pole by the bus stop, in a patch of stinging-nettles. It had always been there and had never been of the slightest interest to anyone at all. Telegraph poles were a bit like that: just *not* exciting things.

But today, Harris stopped and looked at the telegraph pole.

"It says seventeen," he said to Jack.

Jack paused. "There are lots of seventeens in the world, you know, Harris," he said.

"I know there are lots of *other* seventeens," said Harris. "But maybe this is *Timmy's* seventeen."

"I don't see how," said Jack, trampling through the nettles to stare at the pole. On the side of the pole there was a most uninspiring, official-looking sign. It simply stated, '17'.

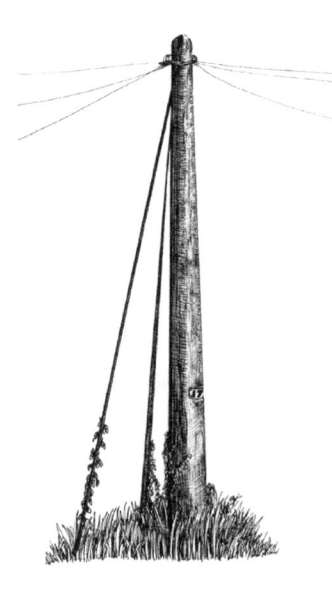

"I expect it's so the people who mend poles and wires and stuff know which one to mend," said Jack, as if he knew far more about the subject than he did. "I expect if there's something broken, someone says, 'Go and fix pole seventeen!'"

Harris giggled. "But in the adventure where you and Timmy met up in the snowstorm, didn't Timmy walk into the land of Err from this bus shelter here?"[5]

Jack stared more closely at the number seventeen on the pole. What if Harris was right? What if there was something about this bit of road, about this normal bus shelter, about this boring telegraph pole in a patch of stinging-nettles, which really did lead to Aletheia? It seemed so very unlikely. It was so *uninteresting* here. Where could there even be an 'underground entry'?

"We'll check the ditch," he decided.

Harris scrambled after Jack through the nettles, around a stray patch of prickly brambles, and down the overgrown banks of the soggy, muddy ditch. Jack picked up a broken stick. He poked the sides of the ditch, whacking nettles and weeds as they pushed through the mass of tangled, annoying vegetation.

It was a surprising ditch. It sloped downwards without seeming to do anything of the sort, until the boys were hidden from the world above. And then Jack stopped suddenly in surprise. Harris bumped into him and tried to see around Jack.

"What is it? What is it, Jack?" he asked eagerly. "Have we found Aletheia?"

"Not Aletheia," said Jack slowly, "but…" He stared at a most unexpected discovery.

At the side of the deep ditch, barely visible through the thick grass and weeds, was a small, wooden door. And on it was a printed number: the number '17'.

It wasn't anything extraordinary. It looked like a place grown-ups might have put normal pipes and wires and stuff to come and mend things. But Jack had a special feeling about this door and he pulled eagerly at the weeds, ignoring the sharp tingly sting from the stinging-nettles. There wasn't any handle on the door that Jack could see, and he and Harris pushed on it together. Slowly, one nudge at a time, the door scraped and creaked open until there was a small space.

"It's a good job you've got your rucksack with you, Jack," said Harris, breathless with excitement at this unexpected development. Jack's rucksack contained what he considered were his 'essential supplies' for the longed-for expedition to Aletheia. It had school stuff in it too, but he didn't care much about that. He was glad he hadn't given up carrying his Bible and other supplies with him.

"I think there's just enough room for me to get in," said Jack, cautiously exploring the narrow opening with his head and shoulders.

"I'll come too," said Harris anxiously.

"I'll go through and explore," said Jack. "You wait here and I'll call to you when I know it's really and truly the Underground Entry to Aletheia."

Harris was not particularly pleased to be left outside of the excitement of exploring beyond the grimy wooden door, but there wasn't, in any case, room for two, and he was accustomed to following orders from Jack.

Slowly, with not a few scrapes on his skin, and no little dirt on his clothes, Jack vanished bit by bit through the wooden door.

Harris waited, listening intently from the dirty ditch. "Is it the Underground Entry, Jack?" he called. "Did we find the way to Aletheia?"

CHAPTER 2
THE SLIDE

Jack did not intend to go far without Harris. There was a small, square, dirty space beyond the door, and, opening from this, a grubby pipe which might just take one small-ish boy. Jack crawled slowly and painfully down the narrow pipe, barely fitting with his rucksack on his back. It was a very small space and there was hardly room to breathe but how he would turn around and get back to Harris did not occur to him. Jack seldom worried about the unknown; as the kids in Aletheia had found, it made him very brave on adventures. The narrow tunnel down which Jack crawled on all fours was disappointingly like a manmade drainage pipe. Until he reached the bend. And then, most unexpectedly, everything changed.

He was suddenly at the entrance of a huge underground cavern, with walls and ceiling of massive rocks. Jack could only dimly see the space around him because of a faint light from a distant source. There was nothing in the cavern, nor did it appear particularly interesting. But there were several other entrances and exits to and from the massive cave: some large, some small, all leading somewhere unknown. Overcome with curiosity, he scrambled to his feet and walked towards the large exit which appeared to be the source of the strange light.

Jack reached the rocky archway leading from the cavern and stared in utter amazement. He was not easily surprised, but nothing could have prepared him for this sight. Before him was simply the most massive hole that could conceivably exist under the earth without everything aboveground tumbling straight into it and being swallowed up! And Jack was perched, like an ant at the top of a mountain, at the mouth of the longest, most terrifying slide imaginable. Down it plunged, into the nothingness below. It was narrow, smooth, gleaming, and absolutely the steepest thing ever.

Before Jack could offer even the smallest protest, the floor on which he stood lurched suddenly and he was plunging down the slide, on the craziest ride of his life. There was no chance to retrace his steps across the cavern and make his way up the too-small pipe to Harris. There was nothing and no one to tell him where under the earth he was, and how in the world he could ever get back again. There was nothing, absolutely nothing, to do but to literally go with the supersonically-fast flow.

Afterwards, Jack could never decide whether that stomach-churning, gravity-defying, completely-out-of-control ride through the massive space of nothingness was the most terrifying thing he had ever done. He had quite a list of experiences from his previous adventures in Aletheia, so it was hard to decide.

Whether the drop through the earth was long or short was hard to tell. It went on and on – but it was so rapid it was quickly over. Jack was ejected abruptly off the end of the slide, onto a surprisingly soft, bouncy mattress which appeared to have been placed there exactly for that purpose. He bounced sharply upwards high into the air and then plunged downwards, again and again, until at precisely the right moment he bounced gently off the mattress and at last onto solid ground again. Then, wonderingly, Jack looked around.

It was not dark or dirty in the heart of the earth. It was not silent or spooky. Jack felt safe, not alarmed. It had the feeling of a place deliberately intended to be exactly where it was: far beneath the ground. He had landed in a small alcove at the side of what appeared to be a street, lit with the kind of old-fashioned, friendly lamps you see on Christmas cards. He had no notion whether this could possibly have been the light he had seen dimly from the cavern. It seemed impossible – and yet it was not.

Slowly and gingerly, Jack got to his feet. High, so high, above him, disappearing into utter darkness, the slide which had taken him to this strange place stretched tall and recklessly steep, apparently unsupported by anything at all. Criss-crossing the vast space were dozens of other slides of different colours, various lengths, and every variety of width and size, all coming to wherever he was, from other locations – wherever they were. Did they all start in uninspiring drainage ditches too…? Perhaps you could reach this place from all around the world.

Not stopping to be perplexed, Jack straightened the rucksack on his back and stepped away from the yawning cavity above him, out of the alcove, and onto the unknown underground street. It was clean and cobbled, with stone and brick buildings along each side. The walls of the buildings were very thick and sturdy. They had the appearance of being foundations. They stretched upwards until they vanished into the rocky, earthy roof which was not too far above the road. Jack wondered if the walls went straight through the ceiling and became proper buildings in the aboveground world.

The lamplight was strong and warm; it was pleasantly balmy for being so far underground. Jack stopped under a streetlight and examined it curiously. Instead of a flame or an electric light bulb – such as he might have expected to see anywhere else in the world – a small book shone brightly from the centre of the glass-encased light: steady, white and warm. It was impossible to see what type of book it was from the street below, but there was only one book Jack had ever known to show such light. And that was the Bible. On his previous adventures in Aletheia and in the wider land of Err, Jack had learned the Bible shone with light. The verse in the Bible about the Word of God being a light[6] came true literally in Aletheia. And, in this underground place, there were undoubtedly books being used to light the streets. But this subterranean world was nothing like the Aletheia Jack knew.

There were tubs of flowers on the street, outside narrow doorways, adding a splash of brightness. They were carefully tended and evidently thrived under the warm streetlight. Jack wandered down the street. A man stepped out of a shop and watered the tub of flowers outside of his door.

"Excuse me, sir," Jack said politely, approaching the man.

The man straightened up. "Good evening to you," he said cheerfully.

Jack read the small sign which was tacked to the door of the shop: 'Proprietor: Mr Nathanael Upright', and the shop was called 'Goodness'. It was a promising start. "Can you tell me where I am, please?" asked Jack.

The man put down his watering can. "Where exactly are you trying to find, son?"

"Well…" Jack considered how to explain. "Where have I come to?"

"This street? This is the Shopping Parade," the man said kindly. "It takes a bit of getting used to, doesn't it?" he added. "Living underground like this."

Jack imagined it would take *a lot* of getting used to living underground, although it didn't seem so bad with neat streets, all lit with the warm, friendly lamps. "Can't you live above the ground?" he asked with interest.

Mr Nathanael Upright stared at Jack. "Live aboveground?" he asked in astonishment. "With this invasion? Don't you know about the plan?"

"Invasion?" echoed Jack. "Plan?"

"Oh, I see!" The puzzlement on Mr Upright's face cleared and he looked at Jack with even greater interest. "Have you come from the Outside?" he asked.

Jack figured the drainage ditch and his own sleepy, uninteresting village of Steeple-Bumpton was definitely 'Outside' of this place. "Yes," he said. "I came down a steep slide."

"It's been a while since we've had any Outside help arriving," remarked Mr Upright. "We need all the assistance we can get!"

Dread was growing in the pit of Jack's tummy. This talk about invasion and living underground, could it really be…? "Is Aletheia at war?" he asked frankly. If the man had no idea what Aletheia was then there was no real harm in asking. But a shop called *'Goodness'* had all the feeling of being in Aletheia.

Mr Upright didn't appear to think Jack had lost all of his marbles at the mention of Aletheia and war. Instead he sighed sadly. "You really have come from the Outside, haven't you?" he said. "Didn't you know? Aletheia has been invaded by Err!"

Jack was appalled. "Is-is…is everybody dead?" he stuttered, horrified at the thought of Aletheia, the mighty city of Bible Truth, overcome by invaders and *actually* defeated.

"Oh, bless you, no!" said Mr Upright. "No casualties on our side, not yet anyway. Unless you count those who have Fallen Away and joined the enemy. Or the folk on The Outskirts, some of whom haven't even noticed the difference! But most of us are safely underground, building up our foundations, strengthening our resources, preparing to defeat our enemies!"

Jack didn't understand Mr Upright's references to 'building up foundations' and 'strengthening resources'. He was trying to take in the drastic changes that must have occurred in aboveground Aletheia over the summer, trying to put together the missing pieces in the jigsaw. "W-was it the Meddlers who did this?" he asked. It seemed to him that somehow the Meddlers, who planned the fall and ruin of Aletheia, had succeeded.

"Yes, the Meddlers' plan was a big part of it," said Mr Upright. "But, of course, the Council of Err and the people of Err, and a whole lot of other creatures of Err are behind it too!"

After further explanation from Mr Upright, Jack understood that it had not taken the Meddlers long to pollute the Water of Sound Doctrine, which was the city's boundary, and all the aboveground water courses too. But there was a far deeper source of water that the Meddlers knew nothing about. What was seen aboveground was the merest hint of the fathomless water that lay beneath the foundations of Aletheia. And so, to protect the source of the water, the city moved underground. It was not difficult. Jack learned that every permitted building in Aletheia had foundations stretching deep and firm and steadfast beneath the ground. The whole of Aletheia was simply replicated below the earth. It always had been. The Goodness shop, indeed all of the shops on the Fruit-of-the-Spirit Shopping Parade, moved their stock to their well-secured basements, and business carried on – almost as usual.

"We can still get aboveground," said Mr Upright. "The buildings are all secured with Bible-access-only, and we guard every window and doorway we possibly can. Our enemies can't see us behind the light of the Bible! It's all hands on deck, and nearly every able-bodied person is on guard duty shifts."

Jack was cheered to think the folk in Aletheia were guarding the old city and that the people from Err hadn't yet penetrated the ancient buildings there or found the hidden underground. "And is-is there a plan to take back the city?" he asked hopefully.

"Absolutely!" said Mr Upright. "We are underground and invisible, but not defeated! We are growing in prayer strength, and one day, very soon, we hope to take back our city and drive out the invaders!"

Jack was most heartened to hear there was talk of taking back Aletheia. "If you meet another boy," he said to Mr Upright in parting, "another boy like me, but smaller, can you send him after me? He's my brother, and he hasn't been to Aletheia before."

"I'd be honoured, I'm sure," said Mr Upright. "I'll keep an eye on the Slide-Landings!"

He watched Jack walk down the street and turn the corner.

CHAPTER 3
UNDERGROUND ALETHEIA

When Jack found out from Mr Upright that the underground city basically replicated the aboveground city, he knew exactly where he was going. And when you looked closely at the foundations of the buildings, they were oddly familiar: as if they bore some resemblance to the rest of the building they supported above.

Just around the corner at the end of the street was Jack's destination: the home of his friends, the Wallops, at Foundation-of-Faith Apartments. Of course, you couldn't see the apartment block towering above most of the other buildings as it did in aboveground Aletheia. Here all the buildings stopped at the rocky, earthy ceiling, so everything was the same height. But when Jack turned the corner he knew he was at the right place. It wasn't that the Wallops' underground home was like the tall, elegant apartment block above the ground, but the massive foundations before him were stately in their own way. There were no doors, instead open archways and tall pillars of huge stones led to a labyrinth of openings and doorways and nooks and crannies. It was a vast network of individual rooms and spaces, with colourful curtains and comfy sofas in odd corners, the smell of dinner cooking, and bright lamplight flickering warmly over the whole scene, making the giant camp appear cheerful and welcoming.

Jack wouldn't have known where to start searching for the Wallop family in the vast foundations, but, at that very moment, a small, scruffy white dog came racing helter-skelter towards him, running joyfully into the freedom which was found on the hidden streets of the city.

"Hector!" shouted Jack.

"Jack?!" Hector's master, Hezekiah – or Zek – Wallop, Jack's very good friend and sharer of past adventures, rushed towards him.

At last, Jack was back in Aletheia.

In the past there was nothing unusual about strangers coming to Aletheia and becoming part of life there. People came – and went – for many reasons, as Jack had found on his previous visits. But this was war, and no one had been able to enter underground Aletheia since additional security measures were put into place to protect against intruders to the hidden city. No one from the Outside had discovered the way to underground Aletheia: apart from Jack.

Mrs Daisy Wallop, Zek's mother, was very pleased to see Jack again. She made him warmly welcome, then rushed away to put together "something special" for tea.

"I don't know how special it will be," said Zek warily. "We're on food rations because of the invasion!"

Jack felt guilty he hadn't carried more of his brother's hidden stores of tins and jars of food in his rucksack. He was glad he had at least brought a supply of biscuits from the kitchen at home – even if they had been liberally sampled by him and Harris.

Zek's father, Mr Hardy Wallop, the Superintendent of Entry to Aletheia, arrived home for tea – still dressed in his smart navy uniform with polished silver buttons. Since he was in charge of all the entries into Aletheia, including Underground Entry, he was particularly interested in Jack's account of his journey to join them. He quizzed Jack about it, especially about the large cavern with lots of exits. Mr Wallop needed to make sure the enemies of Aletheia could not discover the way Jack entered their underground world.

Timmy Trial also listened to Jack's story of his entry to underground Aletheia. Timmy was Jack's friend from his own village of Steeple-Bumpton. Timmy had special permission to be in Aletheia and he lived with the Wallops when he was there. He hadn't been able to get back to his parents in Steeple-Bumpton since the war began.

"I didn't used to come through the drainage ditch," Timmy remarked, when Jack finished his account. "You were pretty smart to think of following the number seventeen on the telegraph pole, Jack."

Mr Wallop didn't say much about the drainage ditch part of the tale. Jack thought he was a bit puzzled at that detail.

"Well, it was really my brother, Harris, who thought of following the number seventeen telegraph pole," Jack explained. He wondered what Harris was doing now. Was he still waiting for him? Or would he find his way to underground Aletheia too?

"We'll have people watching out for your brother in case he joins us," said Mr Wallop. "It all depends what happens when he reaches the large cave you described, you see?"

Jack didn't see at all. "He might follow the light, like I did," he said hopefully.

Mr Wallop's bushy moustache, which made him appear so fierce and forbidding, twitched as he considered the problem of the cavern. Why it was a problem wasn't clear to Jack, or Zek, but Timmy said, "Do you think it could be a breach in our security, sir?" as if he guessed what troubled Mr Wallop.

"I fear so, Timmy," said Mr Wallop. "Perhaps it will be to our advantage if your brother resists our enemies at the cavern, Jack," he remarked. "Perhaps that's why he has remained behind."

Jack said nothing to that suggestion. He didn't point out how small Harris was, and how he hadn't had any experience at all of resisting the enemies of Err. Instead he remembered the lesson he learned from his last adventure, when he and his friends had formed The Mustardseeds[3]: if you had faith in God, even faith the size of a mustard seed, you could do great things[7]. The mustard seed was tiny. It was nothing at all. It was God who was great. It didn't matter how small or insignificant you were; if you placed all of your confidence in God, you could even conquer the foes of Aletheia!

Mr Wallop was not at all surprised at Jack's description of the rest of his journey down the terrifying slide. It was normal for people to arrive beneath Aletheia in that reckless manner.

"The Slide I took used to take me to the Slide-Landing beneath the school," commented Timmy, clearly used to this curious mode of transportation.

Mr Wallop nodded. "Our routes for Outside students are usually precise," he said. "But we mixed up the Slide routes as a way of defending ourselves against any enemies discovering our underground city."

Jack didn't understand how, in this massive underground world, they could block all the entries into Aletheia, although he thought it might explain why he had found it so difficult to find the way. "What have the Meddlers done to the Water of Sound Doctrine?" he asked.

"They have polluted all the aboveground sources of water," said Mr Wallop.

"They sweetened it," said Timmy in disgust.

"They added sugar and syrup and all sorts!" said Zek.

Jack knew, of course, that it was a terrible thing to alter the balanced Water of Sound Doctrine which represented the whole Truth of the Bible. But sweetening it didn't sound so terrible, did it…? "Why is it so very bad that the water is sweet?" he asked.

"Sweetening the water makes it more appealing to the people of Err," explained Mr Wallop. "Instead of trusting in the Lord Jesus, people are trusting in other things to be saved from their sins, such as doing good things or paying money for forgiveness."

"But why wouldn't people want to trust in the Lord Jesus?" asked Jack.

"People always rebel against God and want to do things their own way," sighed Mr Wallop.

"We helped to save some of the crops, Jack!" said Zek.

"You certainly did that!" inserted Mrs Wallop. She placed a plate of hot food on the table for Mr Wallop. He had to eat quickly and get back to his work. There was no rest for the Superintendent in these anxious times.

"If we're careful, we have enough safe food stored to see us through until spring," Mr Wallop explained as he ate his small portion of meat and potatoes. "And that is because you and Zek warned us in time with the Meddlers' Song. Otherwise we might have been watering the Pray-Always crops with the polluted, sweetened water! But instead the farmers watered their crops from our underground reserve of Water of Sound Doctrine, until they could be safely harvested."

Jack was very glad he and Zek had helped save the food supplies for the city. He knew how important it was for the people of Aletheia to eat food watered only by the pure Water of Sound Doctrine.

"There's a plan to retake aboveground Aletheia very soon," said Timmy eagerly.

"We're strengthening our foundations and rebuilding our prayer power," said Mr Wallop. "We're preparing to defeat our enemies and reinstate the Truth!"

Timmy grinned at Jack. "And you're just in time for the action!" he said.

The situation in Aletheia sounded quite heartening the way Mr Wallop described it. They might be living underground with invaders above them in the city, but it didn't sound as if Aletheia was entirely lost.

"Where are Hugo and Henry?" asked Jack, referring to Zek's older twin brother and sister, Hugo and Henrietta Wallop.

"Uh...they were delayed after guard duty at the Academy," said Timmy hastily.

Mr Wallop got to his feet. He had more duties to attend to. "You're very loyal, Timmy," he said drily. "But I am already well aware of Henry's misdemeanour today and why the twins are, uh, *delayed!*"

"Poor Henry!" said Timmy, as Mr Wallop left them and returned to the Academy of Soldiers-of-the-Cross for his never-ending work. "I thought they might not have found out what she did! Hugo stayed behind to support her when she had to see our commanding officer, and I came back here and was going to try and pretend everything was OK!"

"Is it very bad?" asked Zek anxiously.

But it didn't seem so very bad when Timmy laughed. "Well, I understand she overheard one of the officials from Err planning what they would do to gain entry to the Judges' Academy where she was on guard duty," he explained. "She was standing behind the pillars, and the officials from Err were going to mark one of the pillars with paint, so they would know which one to knock down, and Henry was so outraged she threw an apple core straight through the pillars and hit the official right on the nose!"

Zek giggled.

"What did the official do?" asked Jack, trying to imagine this scene. Henrietta Wallop had been part of previous adventures. She was fun, impulsive and courageous and certainly had the capacity to get into trouble.

"Well, they couldn't see Henry at all," said Timmy.

"Couldn't they?" asked Jack.

"It's the light of the Bible," explained Zek. "That's what we guard with, and it blinds people to what's there."

"Oh," said Jack, trying to digest this. It didn't seem possible, but, after all, the Bible was the living and powerful Word of God[8]. Through it, God could do anything!

"Is it Bourne telling Henry off?" asked Zek with interest.

Timmy nodded. "Bourne's in charge of all the volunteer Rescuers – which is what we are," he explained. Jack remembered Lieutenant Bourne Faithful from previous adventures. Bourne was a cousin of the Wallops, a fierce warrior, and a very good friend to have on your side, but Jack would not wish to be in Bourne's bad books!

"So will Henry be in trouble?" asked Zek, anxious for his sister.

Timmy shrugged. "I don't think so," he said, "although I expect

Bourne will make her read *Guard Duty Rules on Discretion and Discovery* several more times! And I don't know what your parents will say!"

Zek grimaced. He could only imagine how his dad, let alone his mum, would view this lapse of security. It was vitally important that the people of Aletheia didn't give away their presence, or their growing power, to their enemies until the time was right and they were ready to fight back. But it was funny to think of the bewilderment of the officials of Err when an apple core came flying out of nowhere, from a place they couldn't get into, and hit one of them on the nose.

Jack enjoyed the story too. It was just like Henry. He imagined what he would feel – watching the old buildings of the city being attacked and demolished by strangers. He would want to throw something too!

CHAPTER 4
ABOVE THE GROUND

High above Aletheia, hidden behind the battlements at the top of the tallest tower of the Academy of Soldiers-of-the-Cross, the leader of Aletheia, Chief Steadfast, looked across the desecrated city of Bible Truth. He was an impressive man of dignity and capability. He was not only in charge of the Academy of Soldiers-of-the-Cross but also of the whole city of Aletheia. On him rested the ultimate responsibility of recovering the city from their enemies and restoring it to peace and safety once more.

The streets of Aletheia were usually deserted at this late evening hour. It had once been the time of peace and tranquillity, when busy Aletheians finished the labours of the day and were at rest. It was a time when you could have heard birdsong and the rustling of trees.

But not now.

Far below, people still walked through the city centre. But these people carried lights and lanterns and poked about them curiously, stopping to peer into the windows, puzzled when they saw light which hid rather than revealed. Occasionally they tried to open a door too. The Chief knew, even if the strangers in Aletheia did not, that the doors to all the buildings in central Aletheia would only open to the touch of the Bible. The buildings in Aletheia were sealed tight against people who did not believe in the Word of God. Nor did the invaders know of the guards stationed behind the Bible-access-only doors, strengthening and fortifying the old timbers with verses of Scripture; they only knew that the doors were unyielding, and actually *stung* anyone who touched them.

But how long would it be before the officials of Err brought in diggers and bulldozers and tried to gain access in other ways? A recent report from Lieutenant Bourne Faithful revealed there were plans afoot, overheard by a guard, to smash a vital pillar at the Judges'

Academy. There was a postscript on the report which almost made the Chief smile: the guard, young volunteer Henrietta Wallop, breached security by throwing an apple core at the official who had voiced the plans. The Chief did not doubt Lieutenant Faithful had dealt with this breach by Miss Wallop and that her father would do likewise. But he had secret sympathy for the action: for which of them was not anxious to drive the invaders from their city?

People from Err were even now busy about the city. A smart, official-looking woman was writing notes on a notepad. A man was taking measurements and making sketches of the buildings crowding onto one of the quaint cobbled streets. There was litter blowing in the chilly autumn breeze – which had never been known in the city before. The flower pots and plants and hanging baskets were sad and neglected, as if they had been hurriedly and suddenly deserted: which they had been. Someone had painted a protest slogan on the walls of the ancient cottages of Election Terrace. Worst of all, in Redemption Square there were the flickering lights of bonfires and some rough, dilapidated shelters where people continued to camp. The camp was a protest. There were banners and flags, and chatter and laughter from the people in the camp wafted up to the Chief on the night breeze. People were still angry with Aletheia for preventing the land of Err from entering the Most Revolting Nation competition earlier in the year[3]. They came to the city to protest against the Truth, and to change it too.

Away from the city centre streets was further devastation. There were campsites scattered across the Pray-Always Farmlands. There were large tents, and caravan-type structures, and big Err Transporters too. The Pray-Always Farmlands were like a massive muddled holiday camp.

In The Outskirts of Aletheia, beyond the farmlands, there glowed the faint glint of gold crosses, representing a different type of message, a new religion that had come over the boundary and settled amongst the people who lived furthest from the old cross in the centre of the city. The Truth of the Bible was being supplanted by something else.

Once the Water of Sound Doctrine was polluted and sweetened by the Meddlers, it was no longer a formidable defence. It no longer showed people the way the Bible saw them – dirty, disgraced, and ruined – in one awful, unbearable reflection. Instead, people were seeing more pleasant, appealing things – so there was no longer any difficulty in people from the land of Err entering Aletheia by crossing the Water of Sound Doctrine.

The Chief sighed and turned away from the sight of the city. He descended from the tower, going deep inside the mighty fortress, along passageways and down stairways, and entered a room which was behind massive, impenetrable stone walls. It was aboveground but not seen, and accessed by the Bible only. In it a group of people sat around a very large, very old table. They were the managers of Aletheia: the people in charge of departments, representatives of all the businesses of Aletheia, heads and directors of everything that mattered in the old city. There were men and women in uniforms with medals, others in smart suits, and the farmer, Mr Croft Straw, conspicuous in his tweed suit with his 'best' cow tie. These people prayed together, and planned together, and fought together for the city of Aletheia.

And now they must plan once more. For, while Aletheia might seem defeated by invaders, all was not lost. Their enemies supposed that the Truth, and everything Aletheia stood for, was what was seen aboveground. They thought the city could be taken as any other city in Err. They were convinced that the Truth could be changed into a new way of doing things, a way more acceptable to the land of Err. They declared a complete victory over Aletheia and flew their flag from somewhere on the Pray-Always Farmlands – while they still puzzled how to gain access to, and fly the flag from, the main city buildings.

They didn't know about the underground resources of Aletheia: the hidden reservoir of Water of Sound Doctrine; the stores of safe

Pray-Always Farmlands food; about the invisible city preparing to rise once more. They didn't know that the Bible was the living and powerful Word of God[8], and that it could not be defeated or changed:

For its power did not come from what could be seen. It was so deep, so invisible, that, without faith, they could never hope to understand it.

CHAPTER 5
MANAGEMENT MEETING

The managers had much to plan before they could re-take the city of Bible Truth and restore it to its former safety and splendour. Crucially, they needed prayer power, and committed Christians, and resources to drive their enemies from the city. The success of the Meddlers was, in part, because the city didn't have enough prayer power to properly defend its boundaries. The managers of Aletheia did not want to make the same mistake again.

The Chief was speaking now, updating the managers about the latest communications from Governor Genie, head of the Council of Err – who was offering terms to the Aletheian people she knew were safely hidden and whom she did not know how to discover. "We've received further correspondence from Governor Genie," explained the Chief, "addressed to me personally, as the so-called 'Leader of Region 15.' She appeals to my sense of…" The Chief withdrew a letter from a neat folder. "Now, what was the exact wording? Ah, here it is. Appealing to my sense of *'justice, love of peace, desire for reconciliation, and shared aim of unity'*…"

Mr Philologus Mustardpot was so outraged he choked on a mouthful of coffee. He was the Head of Education in Aletheia and fiercely loyal to the city. The schools had shut when the city moved underground, and Mr Mustardpot was greatly indignant at the determination of the land of Err to revolutionise Aletheia and destroy the Truth they all held so dear.

"I have also received further news from Outpost Rescuers Mindful and Clarity Markerpen, who, as you know, work in Region 2," continued the Chief. "The Markerpens have been in touch regarding the competition which has now been launched across the land of Err. Naturally, Governor Genie doesn't mention this competition in her correspondence with me."

"Not more *revolting* competitions!" Mr Mustardpot said in an undertone.

"This one is entitled the *Reform Aletheia Competition*…"

Mr Mustardpot snorted very loudly in disgust.

"…which encourages the people of Err to search for, and provide…" the Chief once more read from a piece of paper in his hand. "'*Provide definite proof of the whereabouts of the citizens of Aletheia, leading to their discovery and assistance*'."

He allowed a moment for the disapproving, disgusted murmurs in the room to die down. "The prize is one thousand Erona," added the Chief. "We must expect the lure of money to provoke interest in the many treasure-hunters of the land of Err!"

Mr Mustardpot muttered his own thoughts about the so-called *assistance* of the land of Err which led to Mr Croft Straw, who sat at his side, laughing and almost choking on his coffee too.

"I see this as an act of desperation by the Council of Err," said the Chief. "The Governor already knows we are hidden and might be able to fight back. It's vital we don't drop our guard on the buildings or betray our whereabouts until we have the prayer power to restore the city. Sturdy, perhaps you could now update us on the status and defence of the Water of Sound Doctrine?"

Sturdy Wright, the Head Keeper of the Water of Sound Doctrine, rose to his feet. He was usually a cheerful man with great jokes that made people groan as much as laugh, but the war and the pollution of the aboveground Water of Sound Doctrine had changed that. Now he looked tired and grim. "As you know, all of our aboveground water resources have been sweetened by the Meddlers," he said wearily.

"Is there any danger the polluted, sweetened water can travel through the channels to our underground water reservoir?" asked the Chief.

Sturdy Wright shook his head. "No," he said slowly, "but we must not let down our guard. I'm afraid I still need all the resources that can be spared to stand guard around the water."

The Chief nodded. "It remains our top priority," he assured.

"Nothing must be allowed to pollute the reservoir beneath the cross. We don't want one drop of sweetened water in, otherwise the Truth will be in danger! Not one drop!"

There was a loud "Amen!" from Mr Mustardpot who immediately offered to increase his own share of duties guarding the precious, pure Water of Sound Doctrine.

"You already do your fair share, Philologus," said the Chief. "And we have need of your energies elsewhere." Since the schools shut, apart from some monitoring of the small number of students that remained, Mr Mustardpot spent his time energetically helping various city departments. "I know Croft needs all the help he can get too," added the Chief.

Mr Mustardpot nodded. He was very glad to help his good friend, Croft Straw, with his considerable responsibilities. But he wanted to be aboveground, driving the invaders out of the city, and tearing down the false, gold crosses that had appeared in The Outskirts of Aletheia. This new message that came with the gold crosses belittled all the Lord Jesus had done to provide salvation when He died on the cross. It wasn't at all what the Bible said about how people could be saved and one day be in Heaven[1].

"Croft, if you could update us on food distribution," directed the Chief.

Mr Croft Straw rose awkwardly to his feet, straightening and then loosening his cow tie as if it was suddenly far too tight. He considered himself a simple farmer and never enjoyed being placed in the prominent position of the official Pray-Always Farmlands representative. Added to this, he had been given the responsibility, ably assisted by his friend, Philologus Mustardpot, of overseeing food distribution in the underground city. He had tried to convince another farmer, Mr Silage, to take a turn at being the Pray-Always Farmlands representative, but Mr Silage had been horrified at the prospect. With hindsight and the benefit of insightful comments from his other friend, Dr Theo Pentone, the Director of Health and the Chief Scientist of Aletheia, Mr Straw realised that Mr Silage wasn't perhaps the best replacement. "He smells like his name!" Dr Pentone said frankly. "You'll just have to do your duty, Croft, and anyhow, the Chief thinks you're the best man for the job!" And so, dressed in his best tweed suit, Mr Croft Straw faithfully attended the Management Meetings in the Academy.

"Do you have enough help with food distribution, Croft?" asked the Chief.

"Yes, Chief," said Mr Straw. "Philologus deals with any complaints about food rations…" There was a titter of laughter amongst the assembled at the picture this presented, and Mr Mustardpot smiled.

"And do we still have enough seed to plant safe Pray-Always crops in the spring?" asked the Chief anxiously.

"*No one* will touch the seed!" promised Philologus Mustardpot.

"We have separated our seed supplies from the main food distribution, and Philologus has, uh, devised a safety system for guarding the seed for spring planting," said Mr Straw. "I also have the assistance of a couple of the children," continued Mr Straw. "Zek Wallop…" Mr Wallop smiled. His youngest son's keenness for farming was well-known amongst them: ever since he had put himself at risk to protect the crops last spring. "And Jack Merryweather has also arrived back in Aletheia, to help with the war effort," added Mr Straw.

"Has he?" asked the Chief, considerably surprised.

There were pleased, but astonished, comments amongst them all. They all knew the name Jack Merryweather. Jack had played a vital role, warning the city of the impending attack on the Water of Sound Doctrine. But the news that he had returned was a surprise to nearly all of them.

"Hardy, have you…?"

"I've spoken with Jack, Chief, and his entry to underground Aletheia seems to leave no trail. There appears to be no risk that our enemies could follow," said Hardy Wallop.

"Good," said the Chief, clearly very puzzled, as they all were, how that remarkable boy, Jack Merryweather, could have found his way to their secure underground refuge.

"Uh…" Mr Straw wasn't quite finished. "The boys, that is to say, Zek Wallop and Jack Merryweather, are keen for guard duties at the farmhouses on Pray-Always Farmlands," he said.

The Chief glanced at Mr Hardy Wallop, who shrugged; he knew nothing about this matter. "We need all the help we can get," the Chief said. "I'll leave this matter in your hands, Croft. Do as you see fit, and put them under the charge of, uh, let's see…Lieutenant Faithful, I think."

Mr Straw nodded, considerably relieved to have spoken up for his two young friends and cleared the matter with 'the boss.' He wasn't certain so small a thing should be raised at such an auspicious meeting – except perhaps because it concerned these particular boys: the heroes of the most famous Fretter capture in their times[3].

Captain Steadfast, the Deputy Chief, was the next to give his report. He was dressed in his smart, gleaming, decorated uniform – a considerably more impressive figure than Mr Straw. "As you're aware, we've started training, and putting together a number of attack scenarios for the rescue of the city," said the Captain.

"Good, good…" nodded Mr Mustardpot.

"We've also received a steady increase in rescue requests from The Outskirts," Captain Steadfast continued.

"Never thought I'd see the day!" boomed Mr Mustardpot in surprise.

It was usually so hard helping the Christians who lived in The Outskirts away from the cross. It seemed that nothing affected them or motivated them to return to the cross at the centre of Redemption Square.

"We're making good use of our safe entry points into the Academy," added Mr Wallop. "The light of the Bible is protecting our comings and goings."

"Perhaps our enemy has overreached itself!" suggested Sturdy Wright, looking pleased at last.

"We're rescuing daily, and bringing people from The Outskirts to underground Aletheia," Captain Steadfast confirmed. "It seems the false religion has indeed convinced some Christians to return to their roots, and come back to the cross of the Lord Jesus, who is the only way."[9]

At last there was something to smile about.

"Amen!" said Mr Mustardpot.

CHAPTER 6
JOSIE'S IDEA

Josie Faithful took a brief moment of respite from working at her desk. She got up and went to the window overlooking the secluded street below. The street was blocked entirely at one end by the tower in which she stood – the tower of *The Truth* newspaper offices. The dead-end street was largely untouched by the invaders, but earlier today some officials with clipboards and strange instruments had walked the length of it, taking notes and talking in huddles. They were eyeing the tower too; very likely they had plans, as they did for all of Aletheia, to change it into something that was not *The Truth* at all. Josie shivered. She was safe here – for now. The high windows were carefully tinted to ensure no one could see into the upper floors. On the ground floors there were guards of the Academy of Soldiers-of-the-Cross. But it would not be long, Josie felt sure, before the Council of Err devised other means to enter the city buildings.

She returned to her desk in the small office she was so pleased to call her own. It was meticulously organised, with everything in exactly the right place. She worked hard on her assignments, determined, at all costs, to justify Miss Communique's faith in her. Miss Candour Communique was the young, attractive Editor and boss of *The Truth*.

She had allowed Josie the privilege of doing her favourite thing during the war: organising, and thinking, and noting, and writing, and generally being useful to the staff of *The Truth*. Apart from the awfulness of the war and what it was doing to Aletheia, Josie was delighted to swap school for her role here.

"Still hard at work, Josie?" Candour Communique was standing at the door to the office.

Josie eagerly snatched a neatly drafted report from the right spot on her desk and handed it to Miss Communique. "I've finished the draft you requested," she said.

Miss Communique smiled. She had had the right hunch about young Josie Faithful from the moment she had seen her in the interview Josie and her cousin, Henrietta Wallop, had conducted for the Mustardseeds[3]. Josie was clever, organised, quick-thinking, and a good writer. And now she was helping the hard-pressed staff of *The*

Truth to keep Aletheian citizens up to date with the vital developments in the war against the invaders.

"Uh, Miss Communique..." Josie was hesitant and Candour Communique looked up from the report. "I was wondering...you asked me whether I had any ideas of my own..."

"Yes?" said Candour with interest. So far Josie was merely an extra pair of neat and careful hands to fetch and carry and draft things. But Candour had encouraged her to suggest ideas of her own.

"Well, I was thinking of an article about The Outskirts, you know, with all the people coming back to Aletheia, back to the cross..."

"Yes?" prompted Candour.

"Well, maybe I could, uh, do some research for an article on the rescues taking place there..."

"An excellent idea," said Candour at once. "Although, we must be careful not to tie up our busy Rescuers with interviews and whatnot," she added.

"I was thinking my cousin and his friend, who have done the basic Rescuer training for the war, could perhaps, uh, go out into The Outskirts with the Rescuers and do some research for me? I could put the questions together, and if they would be allowed..."

Candour Communique nodded. She smiled a hidden, secret sort of smile. "I think I know just the man to ask," she said.

Private Harold Wallop, Rescuer-in-training at the Academy of Soldiers-of-the-Cross, was the eldest of the Wallop children. He lived in accommodation at the Academy and worked long hours in this time of crisis, part of a team of Rescuers who were daily going into their besieged city and rescuing people who were praying for help. The Central Control Room located the people who needed help, and everyday Harold and his fellow-Rescuers scanned a list of places to visit, and people to find and bring back to the centre of Aletheia, to the underground refuge beneath the cross. Mostly, Harold worked with his cousin, Lieutenant Bourne Faithful, who was an experienced Rescuer and Josie's eldest brother. But Lieutenant Faithful had other responsibilities too, among which was overseeing the younger volunteer rescuers who would usually be in school attending lessons, but instead, in this hour of need, took shifts at guard duty.

Before Harold and Bourne went out on their rescue missions that morning, Captain Ready Steadfast waved them into his office.

"I've received an, uh, unusual request from Miss Candour Communique, Editor of *The Truth* newspaper," he said.

Harold kept a very straight face and did not dare to glance at Bourne. They knew full well who Miss Candour Communique was. She was an attractive lady, and, if rumour was to be believed, Captain Ready Steadfast was an admirer of hers.

"It relates to a newspaper article that, uh, that your sister, Lieutenant, is involved with."

Bourne nodded. He had not seen much of his family in the last few frantic weeks, but he was aware of Josie's additional responsibilities at *The Truth* newspaper offices. "Yes, sir," he said politely.

"Well, as part of, uh, research for this article, Miss Communique has requested that a couple of volunteers, as, uh, suggested by your sister, be allowed to accompany you on a mission to The Outskirts."

Harold stared at the formidable man who was the Deputy Chief of Aletheia, and head of all the Rescuers. However had Josie managed that? Or was this due to their Captain wishing to please a certain lady? He was amused at the scenario and pleased when Captain Steadfast instructed them to collect the two nominated 'volunteers' for a mission at the first suitable opportunity.

"I'm leaving this matter in your hands. Take all routine precautions as usual – you know the drill," Captain Steadfast instructed. He turned back to the mountain of paperwork by which he was surrounded. There was so much work involved in running an entire city underground, and planning to retake the aboveground city, and rescuing those who at last recognised their need to come back to the cross and the Truth of the Bible. There was a great deal for which the busy Captain was responsible. And that he found time, in his mountain of work, to deal with a minor request from the young newspaper Editor was quite remarkable.

CHAPTER 7
PREPARATIONS FOR A MISSION

Timmy and Hugo, relieved of regular guard duty for an altogether more exciting prospect, walked quickly across the polished floor of the Academy of Soldiers-of-the-Cross.

"Good old Jo!" said Hugo warmly. How his cousin had managed it he had no idea. But somehow she had arranged that they would spend a day with Harold and Bourne, on a real rescue mission, on the streets of aboveground Aletheia! It was not much short of a miracle to be granted such a privilege, and Hugo and Timmy were determined to make the most of it. They hadn't been into open air Aletheia for months, and now they would see firsthand the state of their city.

Following Bourne's instructions, they hurried to the Stair-Gobbler and, as if they were experienced Rescuers, climbed gamely aboard and pulled the control lever around in a neat circle until their destination read, 'Central Control Room'. Then Hugo pushed the big green 'Go' button.

Of course, they weren't experienced Rescuers at all. Hugo had been on this dizzy, wild, stomach-churning, top-speed ride up the stairs of the Academy only once before: at the outbreak of the purple storm[10]. Timmy had never experienced it at all. They were flung around and around the giant, circling staircase at breathtaking speed as the Stair-Gobbler seemed to eat up the stairs on smooth runners. Then, when they least expected it, the Gobbler stopped as quickly as it started, flinging them forward in their seats, halting with minute precision at the small landing space outside the Central Control Room.

Hugo attempted to leap out as unconcernedly as he was certain a real Rescuer would. But he landed on unsteady legs and clutched the handrail close by. Timmy didn't attempt an elegant exit. He staggered out of the Stair-Gobbler, his eyes wide with astonishment, but at least he wasn't sick.

"Jo felt sick after her first ride," said Hugo, gesturing at the 'Sick Here Please' bucket stationed close by.

"I can't imagine why," said Timmy drily.

Hugo grinned. "I hate to think what they do with the sick in these hard-pressed, food-rationed times," he said. They had heard rumours that the contents of the Vomitorium were used as extra animal protein.

They made their way to the big metal door with large silver letters which read 'Central Control Room'. It opened silently as they approached, and they both entered the room and made their way to the balcony, which overlooked the massive circular chamber beneath.

Timmy stared. And stared. And stared.

Hugo grinned. He had been here before but it never failed to amaze him. "Welcome to Dusty's world!" he said.

Timmy spotted their friend, Dusty Addle, amongst the dozens of assorted coloured coats of the Control Room staff. In this time of perplexity and war there were more people manning the machines than ever before. Every clever mind was needed to monitor and record the happenings in Aletheia. "Wow!" said Timmy. "Now I know why Dusty never wants to leave here!"

The complex machines were clicking and clacking, whirling and fizzing, clinking and clanking, spinning and swirling, flashing bright lights, flinging bits of paper, and emitting coloured smoke; one was even raining!

In the corner of the huge chamber, surrounded by people in waterproof clothing, was a see-through water tank with a golden rod in the centre. The golden rod slowly stirred the water and the people anxiously watched the dials and readings on the rod. The water was an unhealthy pink hue; it was clearly not what it was meant to be.

"That's the Water Sensor machine," said Hugo. "They're monitoring the polluted Water of Sound Doctrine. And see? There's Flair!"

Flair Scholar was a friend of theirs from school. She had recently become a Christian[3]. She was very clever and now spent all her spare time working with scientists at the Academy.

Hugo picked up a small speaking tube from beside a screen on the balcony. Then he tapped, 'Speak to Dusty' on the screen. For a brief moment the screen read 'Connecting', and Timmy watched Dusty receive an instruction in his ear and move quickly to the nearest speaking tube in the massive Control Room.

"Hugo!" Dusty exclaimed, his voice coming through clearly. He looked up at the balcony and gave them a wave. "Timmy! You've made it here at last!"

Timmy nodded. "It's pretty cool," he said into the tube.

"We're here on business, Dusty," said Hugo. "But we thought we'd stop and say hello."

"Right you are," said Dusty cheerfully. "Anything I can help you with?" In his time in the Central Control Room, Dusty had learned a great deal of the workings of the wonderful machines and instruments which recorded just about everything useful about Aletheia and the wider land of Err. In these troubled times, Dusty was proving indispensable. He practically lived at the Control Room, assisting the hard pressed manager, Mr Brian Buffer, in any way he could. Dusty was a good friend and a very useful ally to the other children.

"We're heading out on a mission with Rescuers, to The Outskirts," said Hugo.

"Good for you!" said Dusty enthusiastically.

"We've, uh, been instructed to get the latest, uh, updates on conditions around Pride Way," said Hugo, wanting to get everything right for his cousin, and now commanding officer, Lieutenant Bourne Faithful.

"I take it the standard reports will do?" asked Dusty, all efficient business.

"Uh, yes," said Hugo, who didn't know the difference between a 'standard' report and any other type of report. He wished, as he often did, that he was more than a mere volunteer and initiated into *all* the secrets of the Rescuers.

"Right," said Dusty briskly. "The standard reports you'll need for inter-Aletheia missions this week are: Trouble Trace, Rascal Register, Aletheia Alert, and Revealer Device."

Neither Hugo nor Timmy was familiar with the machines that churned out these reports, although they had a great deal of confidence in Dusty's knowledge. They knew about the massive Prayer Power Monitor, which, even from a distance, showed a healthy green colour, indicating good prayer cover. They knew of the Storm Tracker, which tracked and gave alerts on storms across Err, and the fascinating Weather Guide that tracked and monitored all weather. But these other machines were new to both boys.

Dusty dealt with their request personally. He produced the

necessary reports from the machines, and then left the Control Room and joined the boys on the Observer Deck.

"This one," he said, handing Hugo a sheet of paper with lots of squiggles and patterns and only a few words, "this is the result of the Trouble Trace test. The Trouble Trace shows any new trends and problems and so on. We never ran reports like that for Aletheia before, of course, but now all of Err are arriving here…" He broke off with a sigh. "Well, changed times!"

Hugo read the writing which was the summary of all the unknown squiggles on the page. 'High level: mind alteration gimmicks…' and there followed a list of other matters, all of which were associated with the invaders and the changes they were making in Aletheia.

"The report from the Rascal Register isn't that surprising," said Dusty matter-of-factly. "About what you'd expect really. Meddlers, Sloths, Snares, Stumbles, not too many Fretters yet – it seems they were well and truly blitzed by Jack and Zek[3]! But they're on the rise again!"

It was awful to think that so many of the creatures of Err were now easily crossing the polluted boundary into Aletheia. But neither Hugo nor Timmy wanted to admit that they had not encountered many of the creatures on the list in the past – they only had experience of Meddlers and Snares.

The Aletheia Alert machine was high on almost everything, which was no surprise, and the Revealer Device showed the new inventions of the land of Err which were in the vicinity.

Hugo and Timmy thanked Dusty for their reports and left to once more enjoy the crazy ride on the Stair-Gobbler. Hugo pulled the lever in the Gobbler to 'Armoury'. One thing the reports from the Central Control Room proved for sure:

For this mission in aboveground Aletheia, they would definitely need the protection of their armour of God[11].

CHAPTER 8
ON A MISSION!

Hugo and Timmy reached the armoury of the Academy of Soldiers-of-the-Cross and hastily donned their armour of God[11]. Then the boys followed Bourne and Harold down a small, hidden, winding staircase which led from the Academy onto a narrow backstreet of Aletheia. They held their Bibles in their hands. The light of the Bible safeguarded the hidden entries to the fortress; no one from the land of Err could see them come and go – the light of the Bible blinded the eyes of those who did not believe.

To start with, the stone walls and narrow alleyway were reassuringly normal. It was great to be outdoors again. It had been raining recently and there was a stiff breeze blowing across the city. It felt cold after the constant, mild underground temperature. The boys had last been on Aletheia's streets when the late summer sun was still kind and warm. But now there was the sniff of winter in the air.

They tried very hard not to stare when they left the sheltered alleyway and stepped onto a main thoroughfare of Aletheia. They had seen a little of aboveground Aletheia when they were on guard duty, but here was a very different city. Streets they knew well were being torn up and replaced. Roads were being widened and straightened, and old cobbles ripped up and replaced with an ugly smooth surface. Beautiful, big trees, dressed in the last of autumn colours, were cut down and being chopped up. Close by, a team of people were sawing logs. It was very odd and disconcerting to see so many strangers wandering the streets. There were people making sketches, writing notes, and scanning maps. An artist with an easel was painting a picture of the Academy of Soldiers-of-the-Cross. The picture was weird and distorted and depicted clouds of aliens ascending from or descending onto the top tower of the Academy. A group of men and women, in official-looking suits, were measuring the ancient, terraced buildings of Faith, Hope and Charity up the street, as if they disapproved of their current solid, simple state. A bedraggled, grimy snack stall called 'The Greasy Cook', run by a man with scruffy, tangled hair – who did, indeed, appear to *be* the greasy cook – was situated outside of the dignified but now utterly silent Judges' Academy. It was doing very well feeding all the visitors and workers that had invaded Aletheia. A gang of teenagers were eating hotdogs and sausage rolls at the stall, and idly speculating about the city.

"Where do *you* think all the Aletheian people have gone, Jerry?" asked a girl with purple hair who was eating a hotdog.

"Who knows?" replied the one called Jerry. "They could be invisible!

Chapter 8: On a Mission! 75

Perhaps their powers make them magic!"

"I don't think there's much that's magic about them!" said another.

"I think they fled as soon as real civilisation arrived!" said a boy.

"I think they went underground," said the girl. "Just sank beneath the ground!"

The others laughed.

"Hey, you!" shouted the girl with the purple hair.

Timmy looked around, startled to be singled out.

"You look as if you know your way around here," said the girl. "Do you know how to get to the centre of the city?"

"Follow the cross," said Timmy.

"Thanks," said the girl, looking up, for the first time, to see the cross. "I didn't notice the cross," she said. "I wonder why it's there! Do *you* know where all the Aletheian people have gone?"

"Yes, I know," said Timmy, "but it's a secret."

The gang of teenagers all laughed. They moved onwards into the city.

Harold and Bourne kept walking without showing any concern at the conversation.

"I didn't know what to say," muttered Timmy. "I didn't give anything away, did I? Can they see we're Aletheians?"

"They're just guessing and speculating," said Bourne quietly. "There's plenty of talk in the land of Err about what's happened in Aletheia, and there's a competition called the Reform Aletheia Competition to encourage people to search for Aletheians."

"But they can't see we're Aletheians just by looking at us," added Harold. "They can't see our armour of God[11] or tell where we're from."

"Although we might look less likely to come from Err than some of them!" said Bourne drily, gesturing to the girl with purple hair. "But remember, a few of the people invading Aletheia will want to know the Truth," he added. "Sometimes it's the most unlikely ones. You were right to send them to the cross. The message of the cross of the Lord Jesus[12] will always have an effect on someone who is genuinely seeking the Truth, even though there are protesters there!"

Neither Timmy nor Hugo could see much sign of people seeking. The folk they passed weren't coming to Aletheia to find out the truth the Bible presented about the Lord Jesus being the only way of salvation[9]. They appeared to be in Aletheia for one reason only: to take over and ruthlessly change the city into the mould of the land of Err.

No one took any notice of the group of two Rescuers and two boys. They walked down Pride Way. Ahead of them, the pleasant rural landscape of Pray-Always Farmlands was dramatically changed. Gone were the rolling, well-kept fields of the farmlands. Orchards, and scattered trees that sheltered barns and farmhouses, were cut down and destroyed. The barns and houses themselves were abandoned and empty. Fields, which should have been ploughed and lying quietly and contentedly bare over the winter months, were home to Transporters, and tents, and accommodation for the invading people who were now in Aletheia. Some looked like they had come to live for a while. There were rough shelters constructed here and there, and small bonfires by the shelters, gradually consuming the once-fragrant branches of the Pray-Always fruit trees.

The big Transporters of Err were more official-looking. They were home to the Err officials who went about the city of Aletheia surveying and measuring and planning the changes, and trying to work out how to get into the buildings in central Aletheia that so stubbornly refused to yield to them. To Hugo and Timmy it seemed they would complete an entire takeover of the city at any moment. So much had changed so quickly! Was there any way it could all be put right again? Or was the city already lost?

Pride Way was muddled with workers from 'Err Transport' who were digging up the steep road and replacing it with a 'Moving Staircase' which would take people easily to the top of the road. They were all too busy to notice the party of four who were picking their way through the tools, and materials, and even through the tents at the side of the road. Timmy was certain he spied Plod, an Err Transport Monitor he met on a previous adventure[5]. Plod was taking a prolonged tea break and watching other people work. Timmy felt sure that this was the final convincing evidence that it was Plod: it was just what Plod was likely to do.

When they reached the gates of Law Villas, the two Rescuers went on to collect a party of praying people and left Timmy and Hugo to carry out the 'research' they had agreed with Josie. The two boys had been to The Outskirts before the takeover of Aletheia, when the Meddlers were attacking the crops, back in the spring[3]. They hadn't made any headway with the people at Law Villas then. People who lived away from the cross didn't seem to worry about the things that concerned other Christians of Aletheia, and the folk at Law Villas frankly didn't seem to care about anything but rules and regulations.

The regimented black and white buildings at Law Villas were built to precise measurements and all looked exactly the same. There were dozens of neat black and white signs which displayed rules and instructions for everything you could possibly think of. But when Hugo and Timmy approached the gates they realised there were changes here too. The big, black, shiny gates were shut tight, and around Law Villas was a new, high wall, outside of which was planted a fast-growing, thick, prickly hedge. At the gates there were new signs that weren't remotely welcoming. 'Invaders Keep Out', read one; 'If You Don't Like Rules Go Away!' stated another.

"I suppose, strictly speaking, that includes us," said Hugo, contemplating the high, shut gates. "We don't like their rules!"

"But we're here on a mission," said Timmy. "We need to get information for Jo's article."

Hugo nodded. "We'll have to try," he conceded. Neither of the boys wanted to let Josie down, especially when she had been good enough to organise this mission.

They tried to open the gates, because it seemed stupid not to at least check if they opened. But of course they didn't yield. Instead, to their surprise, the monotone voice of a machine said, 'Please clean your prints off our gates!'

Hugo glared at the gleaming, spotless black gates. "Aletheia is in a state of ruin and all *they're* worried about is *fingerprints on their gates!*" he said indignantly.

"They've got to be the nuttiest people in Aletheia," remarked Timmy.

"I wonder how we can get in," said Hugo gloomily. They had not anticipated this obstacle, and there was an hour to fill before they were due to meet up with Harold and Bourne again.

Suddenly Hugo was aware of something in the prickly hedge close by. He peered into the dense, unfriendly thorns and wicked, twisted branches. What he saw made him go very still.

Someone was watching them.

CHAPTER 9
DIM VIEW

Hugo looked closely at the strange apparition which was in the middle of the prickly bush. "Speaking of nutty people," he muttered to Timmy, "I think we've got one right here!"

Timmy, too, peered into the thicket. "Uh, are you OK in there?" he asked, unable, for the moment, to think what else to say. The old man, who seemed to be moulded to the unkind prickles of the bushes, must be exceedingly uncomfortable.

The strange eyes, which appeared to be encased in swimming goggles, blinked in confusion. "Are-are-are you-are you…" the old man stuttered. "Are you *Christians?*"

Hugo pulled back a couple of the thorny branches to see the man. "Of course we are," he said, forgetting for the moment that Aletheia was now full of people who weren't Christians and didn't believe in the Bible at all. "What on earth are you doing in there?" he asked.

"I can s-see y-your armour," said the old man.

"Then you know we're Christians," said Hugo briskly, "and you must be one too. Where's *your* armour?"

"L-lost," said the old man. "M-m-many years lost. But I found m-my Bible!" He grasped eagerly at the old Bible which was hidden in the prickly bush beside him.

"I think you'd better come out," said Hugo, watching the thorns scratch the man whenever he moved.

It wasn't a very comfortable process, but the old man was eventually free of the enfolding thorns and branches and stood timidly before the two boys. "Dim View at your service, sirs," he said courteously.

It was very difficult not to stare at the oddity that was Dim View. He had taken every eccentric precaution to be camouflaged – mud-smeared cheeks; twigs and autumn leaves in his hair; weird, distorting goggles over his eyes; a green jump-suit which might have once belonged to a soldier; and the addition of an old, battered Bible which was secured in a pouch and hung from his belt.

"Why were you hiding?" asked Timmy.

"They've o-o-overthrown the city," said Dim View in a thin, trembling voice. "We mustn't be seen!"

Hugo considered that Dim View would certainly attract attention in his current attire. But now was not the time to mention that. "You'd be safe in your armour of God,"[11] he remarked. "You could get some from the armoury at the Academy of Soldiers-of-the-Cross."

The old man's eyes filled with tears. "But it's gone," he said, "everything has fallen! Woe upon us for our endless iniquities! The end has come!"

"No, it hasn't," said Hugo stoutly. "Do you think the Truth is so easily overthrown?" He knew that the truth of the Bible could withstand any storm, but, even so, it was hard to be firm when he could hear the sound of digging, and machinery, and the voices of workers who were even now very close by, digging a different road into Aletheia.

"If only I could know," said Dim View forlornly. "We thought we were safe on The Outskirts, away from the cross – plenty of people live out here! No one bothered us before!"

"It's never safe away from the cross," said Hugo.

"But when the invasion came...the gold crosses...the awful changes they're making! Dreadful, terrible days! That I should live to see the day when all is lost!"

"Why didn't you come underground to safety beneath the cross?" asked Timmy.

"We couldn't get underground like the folks up there!" Dim View gestured towards the centre of Aletheia, high on the hill above them. "We don't know the way!"

"Where do you live, Mr View?" asked Hugo. It was clear the old man did not live at Law Villas. Apart from the fact that he was shut out, he would have broken a dozen rules and regulations with his homemade attire!

"I live at N-No-Witness Apartments," said Dim. "But we want to find the way back to safety beneath the c-cross!"

"There are people in The Outskirts who *want* to come back to the cross?" asked Hugo slowly. It was one of the very questions on their survey sheet, but suddenly and most unexpectedly, instead of conducting a survey, they had become involved in a real, live rescue! They knew Rescuers were rescuing people in Aletheia, but they didn't know how many Christians from The Outskirts were coming back to the cross.

"Y-yes," said Dim excitedly. "Yes-yes, that's exactly it! And that's why I'm here, you see!"

Timmy didn't think it precisely explained the bizarre camouflage. "You were out searching for a Rescuer to take you underground to safety?" he asked slowly and distinctly. It was by no means certain that Dim View was entirely in his right mind.

"Exactly, young s-sir!" said Mr View.

"You could have prayed for help, you know," said Timmy.

"Oh, we did that too!" said Mr View earnestly.

"Well, we can, uh, we can help you," said Hugo. "We're with Rescuers, who have gone to rescue others who have been praying for help."

Tears trickled down the mud-spattered cheeks of Dim View, leaving a trail like a snail. "You're q-quite sure it's s-s-still s-safe beneath the cross?" asked the old man.

"Quite sure," said Timmy. "The damage is all aboveground. Underground, in the foundations, everything is secure."

"S-secure," repeated Dim View. "I'll be secure! And I'll n-never leave the cross again!"

"Well," Hugo cleared his throat, feeling the importance of this momentous event – his very first rescue. "Well, we'll get in touch with the Rescuers, and, uh, arrange to return to Aletheia."

"What about my friends?" asked Dim View anxiously. "Will we rescue them now too?"

"Well," said Hugo again, and once more he cleared his throat to cover his uncertainty.

"I don't see why not," said Timmy eagerly. "We could, you know, Hugo," he added. "We could collect Mr View's friends, and still meet up with Harold and Bourne here again."

Chapter 9: Dim View 87

Hugo hesitated, his hand on the Remote Talker through which he could reach his brother, Harold. It was quite a trek across the Pray-Always Farmlands to reach No-Witness Apartments, but, if they were quick, they could just about manage it in the hour that remained before they were due to meet up once more with the Rescuers. Hugo sighed. He wished he had the authority to act without reference to a real Rescuer, but he knew he should not. He pressed the button on the Remote Talker and held it to his mouth.

"Harold? Hugo here, over."

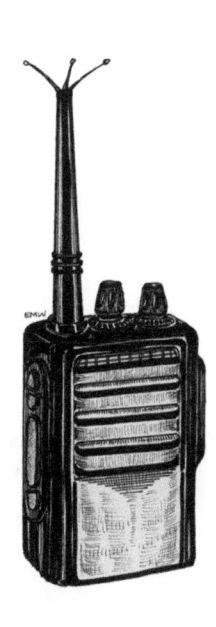

"Hugo…" Harold's response was crackly and unclear.

"Harold, just to update you: we've rescued a man called, uh, Mr Dim View, and we're heading to No-Witness Apartments to collect his friends too. We'll be back at Law Villas soon. Over?"

Hugo…go…doubtful…stumble…farmlands…Aletheia…"

"What does that mean, young sirs?" asked Dim View anxiously.

Neither Hugo nor Timmy had any idea what it meant.

"Well…" said Hugo.

"I think we should go," said Timmy, "and we can update Harold on our way. If we don't start now…"

Hugo nodded. The dim day was quickly fading into grey drizzle and the afternoon was moving swiftly towards evening. If they didn't leave now, they wouldn't be able to go at all.

CHAPTER 10
ENEMY TERRITORY

Walking across occupied Aletheia was a strange experience. It was hard to come to terms with all the drastic and sickening changes. And it didn't help that Mr Dim View, so pathetically grateful and reliant upon his youthful rescuers, was full of sad, grim forebodings, and was, in addition, rather conspicuous to all the workers and other invaders they could not avoid.

"Are you from the circus, dearie?" asked a kindly woman who was taking in damp washing from outside of her homemade shack.

"C-circus?" stuttered Dim View, scuttling closer to Hugo.

Timmy artfully turned an inadvertent, startled laugh into a loud cough.

"The circus," the woman said patiently. "There's one camped at the edge of the city. Didn't you know there's a circus there?"

"Oh, such wickedness and iniquity," muttered Dim View despairingly, plucking at Hugo's arm.

The woman looked dubiously at the strange trio skirting her makeshift camp. "You take care of your grandpa, young man," she said. "I don't think he's right in the head!"

"We'll take care," said Hugo stiffly, and quickly pulled Dim View away. Although they had had their doubts, neither Hugo nor Timmy realised how much attention Dim View would attract on the invaded farmlands. Hugo was beginning to be thankful that there was a circus currently within the boundaries of Aletheia. It meant there was at least one reason Dim View might look the way he did. But none of that explained why it was also so hard to walk across the fields. Every step was becoming a struggle, and the journey they hoped to accomplish quickly was becoming a nightmare.

When they came across the teenage girl with the purple hair, and her gang of friends, sitting under a tarpaulin at their campfire, drinking dubious-looking liquid from plentiful bottles, Timmy's heart sank. It was exciting being part of a real-life rescue, even if it had landed right in front of them without any instigation on their part. But Mr Dim View, with all his considerable peculiarities, was, Timmy privately thought, becoming a liability. Not to say an embarrassment. Probably Hugo thought so too. He pulled Dim View by the arm, trying to manoeuvre him past the camp of teenagers.

"It's the boys from earlier!" said the girl with purple hair. "Hey! You! What's your name?"

Timmy waved a hand in silent acknowledgement, hoping they would leave them alone. He stumbled. It was weird how much they stumbled on the soggy, untended fields. Dim View in particular was constantly unsteady now.

They heard the laughter of the teenagers. "Let them be, Crystal," said one of the boys. "It looks like they're going to the circus!"

"Hey!" Crystal, the purple-haired girl, was coming after them. "Are you?" she asked.

"Are we what?" asked Hugo shortly.

"Are you going to the circus, of course!" said Crystal. "I think it's shut tonight anyway. They had an influx of Meddlers, or something!" she laughed.

"You believe in Meddlers?" asked Timmy with surprise. Many of the people of Err refused to acknowledge the creatures that constantly plagued them. They blamed their troubles on other things instead.

Crystal shrugged. "Why wouldn't I believe in Meddlers?" she said.

"Did you find the cross?" asked Timmy.

Hugo stumbled and Dim View clutched at him. "What is it about the ground…?"

"Stumbles are everywhere," said Crystal, "if you believe in them!"

"Oh, we believe in them alright," said Hugo grimly. He remembered they had been warned of them earlier by one of Dusty's reports from the Control Room. It was just that they had never experienced them before, and now the easy rescue mission was becoming a disaster. They were struggling across Pray-Always Farmlands as the afternoon faded away and the time they had left before they were meant to meet Bourne and Harold ticked away too. And now they were shadowed by one of the invaders of Aletheia!

"What about the cross?" Timmy asked Crystal. He was thinking of what Bourne had said earlier about it sometimes being the most unlikely ones who turned to the cross and trusted in the Lord Jesus for salvation.

"We found the cross," said Crystal. "There's a protest camp there."

"But it's still the cross," said Timmy. "It represents what the Lord Jesus did when He died so that people could have their sins forgiven."[12]

"What about the gold crosses?" asked Crystal. She began walking with them across the farmlands. She ignored the calls from her friends to come back to the fire. "They say that if you give money for the gold crosses God will forget all the bad things you've done and make you rich and happy," said Crystal.

"That's not what the Bible says," Hugo said sternly.

"Oh, that I should live to hear such things!" mumbled Dim View in despair.

"I *thought* you were Aletheians!" exclaimed Crystal. "Only real Aletheians believe all of the Bible!"

Timmy wondered what awful, twisted message the people who were now aboveground in Aletheia believed. Did they no longer believe the Lord Jesus was the only way to be right with God?[9] From what Crystal said, a different message, one about an easier, more appealing way, had been introduced. What *was* happening to the Truth for which Aletheia stood?

Hugo looked with concern at his watch. The deadline for meeting the Rescuers was now past. The Remote Talker bleeped cheerfully in his pocket, too loud to ignore. It penetrated the patter of rain and the murmur of voices from the campsites around them.

"Is that the Rescuers?" Dim View asked hopefully. He was wet and cold, and while he did not for a moment lose faith in his young rescuers, he was longing to reach the promised safety of Aletheia.

The journey across the Pray-Always Farmlands was proving unusually long and tiring. It was like walking through sticky glue. Dim View didn't know anything about the creatures called Stumbles. He had been hiding so long he didn't know how to fight the creatures of Err.

"The Rescuers?" echoed Crystal, picking up on Dim View's remark. "You really are Aletheians!"

"Why are you searching for Aletheians?" asked Timmy.

"You don't know about the competition in Err?" asked Crystal. "You know, the Reform Aletheia Competition! There's lots of money for the person who can prove what happened to the Aletheians! But none of us know what you look like! I mean…" She eyed Dim View with interest, as if the old man, in his startling attire, might be the clue.

"M-money for betraying Aletheia!" said Dim View indignantly. "S-such w-wickedness!"

"Wickedness?" repeated Crystal. "You are totally bats, aren't you? There are plenty of people wanting to claim the prize! And they only want to help Aletheia!"

Feeling very anxious, Hugo slowly pressed the button on the persistently bleeping Remote Talker which could no longer be ignored. He needed Harold's help, no matter the consequences: even if it meant talking in front of Crystal, with her mission to find and betray underground Aletheia. "Hugo? Hugo? Come in, Hugo?"

Harold's reassuringly calm tones came loud and clear through the Remote Talker, across the bleak farmlands.

"I'm here, Harold," said Hugo wearily.

"What *is* that thing?" asked Crystal. "It's pretty cool!"

"Hugo?" asked Harold uncertainly. "Do you have company?"

"Yes," said Hugo.

"What's your current location?"

It was hard to tell. They had been stumbling across the Stumbles now carpeting the Pray-Always Farmlands for…how long was it? How far had they come?

"We're on Pray-Always Farmlands…"

"Yes?" prompted Harold.

Hugo felt miserable. He had no idea where they were. Never, in his wildest dreams, had he imagined he could get lost within the boundaries of Aletheia.

"We're not far above the DIY Centre," said Crystal cheerfully, an unexpected source of help.

"Received," said Harold briefly. "Stay put. On my way."

"Can I meet more of you?" asked Crystal.

"More of who?" asked Timmy.

"Aletheians! Are there lots more of you? Where do you all live? I need to know!"

Timmy thought it would be useful to know more about this competition to reform Aletheia. It might even be of interest to print in the newspaper column, to warn the rest of the underground city. Were the managers of Aletheia fully informed about such things?

"Uh, what exactly is this competition?" he asked.

"The Council of Err want to discover what happened to the people of Aletheia," explained Crystal. "I think they want to help them." She shrugged. She hadn't considered why the Government of the land of Err were interested in finding the people of Aletheia.

"What do you have to do?" asked Timmy.

"They think the people are *still* here somewhere," said Crystal in a hushed tone. She was darting uncertain glances at Dim View. She clearly thought the old man might be more of an Aletheian than Hugo and Timmy – who looked nothing like the alien species that were thought to be the true Aletheians. "There's *one thousand Erona* for the person who has positive proof of where the Aletheian people have gone!"

"Which will probably fly away," said Timmy drily, referring to the prize money of Err. In the land of Err, if people loved money and riches too much, it grew wings and flew away[13]. People invented all sorts of ways of trying to catch and keep it.

Crystal laughed. "Oh, it'll come in weighted treasure boxes, of course!" she said. "But do you know where all the people are?" she persisted.

"You need to search for answers at the cross," said Timmy. "That's the place to start."

"The cross!" echoed Crystal. "You keep going on about the cross! What? Are all the Aletheians hidden there?"

Timmy thought she was surprisingly near the truth. For all true Aletheians – those who trusted in the Lord Jesus as the only way of salvation – always started at the cross. And beneath the cross was the only real place of safety.

CHAPTER 11
HAROLD TO THE RESCUE

Harold was alone when he appeared through the fading light. Bourne was already making his way back to the city, leading a group of people to the safety of underground Aletheia. Harold joined Hugo and Timmy and old Dim View, who was now shivering violently in the chilly autumn air. Crystal was no longer with them. She had reluctantly returned to her friends at their camp.

Harold frowned at Dim View's appearance, but the old man didn't seem to notice. "An honour to meet you, sir," said Dim, bobbing his head and looking at Harold with suitable awe. "These good boys rescued me! Some of us from No-Witness Apartments want to get back to the safety of the cross!"

"You could have waited at home," Harold said kindly. "You didn't need to go out, uh, *disguised*." He glanced once more at Dim View's weird clothing. The old man's appearance was a reflection of what happened when people didn't keep near the cross and do things the way the Bible said. Dim View would have been safe in the armour of God[11], but dressed in disguise his own way, he didn't fit in anywhere at all and was open to attack, even by the creatures of Err. "We received your prayer signal," Harold continued, "and Rescuers were despatched to rescue you all this afternoon. I expect the others are safely underground by now."

Hugo groaned faintly. He was feeling weary and defeated and guilty that Harold had had to come to *their* rescue, instead of helping Bourne. Hugo had thought it so important to set off and collect Dim View's friends as soon as possible. It seemed an easy thing to journey across the farmlands to collect them. But he realised now that he wasn't prepared in the way an experienced Rescuer was.

"It was me who urged Hugo to go and get Mr View's friends," said Timmy, determined to stick up for his friend.

"Never mind," said Harold. "No harm done. No doubt you've got some information from your trip across the farmlands – for your research for Jo's newspaper article!" He was teasing them, but the two boys cheered up considerably. They had, after all, got plenty to tell Josie.

"Who was the girl?" asked Harold.

"She's called Crystal," said Hugo. "She was the girl with purple hair we saw earlier."

"She was on a camp with some friends and saw us passing," added Timmy. "She was asking questions about what happened to all the Aletheians, because she wanted to win the Reform Aletheia Competition and collect the prize money."

"What did you say?" asked Harold.

"I didn't know what to say," said Timmy. "I told her to search for answers at the cross."

"That's always a good answer!" said Harold. He held his Bible in his hand, and the strong light that shone from its pages[6] showed them the way to take, without treading on the Stumbles who made weird muffled squeaking and squelching sounds as they fled from the path before them. He led the bedraggled party by safe, Stumble-free paths back up the hill to the centre of Aletheia once more. Hugo felt ashamed all over again. He had not thought to use his Bible to show them the way across the littered Pray-Always Farmlands. He was trying so hard not to be noticed that he forgot the power of the living Word of God[8].

"It's always safe to use your Bible," Harold explained. "The light of the Word of God will never betray Aletheia, and it can even hide you from enemies, not reveal you to them."

Harold pointed out other creatures of Err too. It was horrifying to Hugo and Timmy to realise how many creatures were following the people across the polluted boundaries of Aletheia. Not only had people invaded the city, but the wicked creatures of Err also made themselves at home there. There were Snares – vague, shadowy creatures with scary, glittering eyes. They lingered in considerable numbers around the numerous campsites, following the people camping there. There were Meddlers too, hovering like swarms of large flies, bugging and plaguing people whenever they could. And Sloths – settling in clouds over various tents and shelters, and in particular over a large encampment which had a colourful banner advertising 'Meditation and Dream Interpretation'. Mysterious music floated across the fields which had once sounded with birdsong. Timmy noticed a large purple marquee on the edge of the site – with a sign which read 'Wander Palm's Prophetic Mystery Telling'. It reminded him of his first adventure in Aletheia, with Jack[2]. Back then, Wander Palm and her prophecies would never have been able to cross into Aletheia. But so much had changed so quickly, and now Ms Palm travelled easily over the polluted boundary and set up her false prophecies on land which had once been farmed by hardworking Mr Silage.

"If you don't bother guarding the Truth, anything will get in," said Harold.

"Woe is me!" sighed Dim View.

"That's what's happened on The Outskirts," said Harold. "People on The Outskirts lived away from the cross and didn't care enough about safeguarding the Truth."

"Our iniquities have come upon us," agreed Dim View woefully.

"Well, the good thing about it is that it's turned sincere Christians back to the true Bible message about how God can justify[14] people only because of what the Lord Jesus did when He died at the cross!"

"Based on Justification[14]," said Dim View, proving surprisingly well-informed. "The true message of salvation is always based on justification by God!"

At last they reached the edge of central Aletheia where the Err Transport workers had packed up for the day and something of the old peace of Aletheia reigned. Harold assisted Dim View down a barely visible alleyway to a small back door of the Academy of Soldiers-of-the-Cross.

They had reached safety at last.

CHAPTER 12
AN IMPORTANT REQUEST

It was hard to imagine that above the rocky ceiling of underground Aletheia the city was overcome by invaders. Here, beneath the city, Jack thought it was exciting to walk along the calm, lamp-lit streets with his friends, part of a hidden, secret world. There was no sound of the outside world, no wind or rain, no birdsong or rustle of plants and trees. There was only the muffled sound of human voices, the faint noise of machinery working, the clink and chatter of household chores and families at home. The shops they passed had doors and windows in their foundations. The hotels and houses opened onto the streets, much like Foundation-of-Faith Apartments. Friends called to each other. Underground Aletheia was safe and cheerful and organised.

"We can camp out some nights," Zek informed Jack as they made their way across the underground city. "There's no weather down here, you see, no rain or anything! And it's always the same temperature, not too hot or too cold at night. Once I was allowed to sleep by the cattle pens," he added, his tone indicating that this was the greatest privilege of all.

Zek wanted to be a farmer and spent as much time as he possibly could helping with the animals who were also living underground.

Jack had similar interests. Back in his home village of Steeple-Bumpton, Jack's grandad was a farmer and Jack loved nothing better than farm work.

They followed the sign which said, 'Cattle Pens This Way'. They could already hear the hollow echo of cows mooing. Zek, and now Jack, worked very hard in the cattle pens in underground Aletheia. There was never a shortage of jobs to do and the boys were always welcome. They mucked out stalls, refilled water troughs, carried clean hay and straw to the pens, and poured bags of dry cattle feed into the feeding troughs. Zek confided that he had heard that the contents of the Vomitorium in the Academy of Soldiers-of-the-Cross were being used to supplement cattle feed. Jack wasn't sure whether to believe that but he dealt very cautiously with the cattle feed following Zek's revelation. He sincerely hoped it was never used for human consumption!

Mr Croft Straw, the important and busy Pray-Always Farmlands representative in Aletheia, was a good friend to the two boys. "Mr Straw," Zek called when he spotted their friend passing by. "Did you remember…?" he asked hesitantly, knowing how occupied their farmer-friend was these days. Had he remembered their all-important request?

Mr Straw came across to the boys at once. "I remembered alright," he said. "In fact, I was looking out for you! You've been granted guard duty at the farmhouses, and I think, perhaps, since you know the layout, you'd better start with mine. Report to Lieutenant Faithful when you're ready to take on your duties!" He saluted them with a twinkle in his eye. "No big adventures, mind," Mr Straw added with a smile. "We had quite enough of them the last time!" He glanced at the scars both boys still bore on their hands. Zek had a two-pronged mark from a deep Fretter bite, and Jack's hands bore the imprint of many poisonous bites[3]. They had baffled the doctors back home, but that did not concern Jack in the least. To him they were the marks of a very great battle for a most worthy cause. They were the cost of standing up for the Truth. And Jack was secretly glad he had something to show he was associated with Aletheia.

Hector, Zek's dog, was as delighted as his master that they were going aboveground to guard a farmhouse. He had no idea, of course, what Zek was talking about, but Hector didn't take much persuading when it came to excitement.

Jack was particularly pleased that he would get to see Fly, Mr Straw's clever black-and-white collie. He was very fond of Fly, and since Jack had learned that Fly still lived aboveground, he wondered how she survived among all those strangers, and whether she had enough to eat – despite being reassured by Zek that there were now so many Meddlers aboveground Fly would be growing fat on them.

"We'll go to Bourne at once," Zek said eagerly. "Perhaps he'll let us go to Mr Straw's house this very night!"

Lieutenant Bourne Faithful was frankly sceptical at the idea of sending Jack and Zek into the war zone, albeit to one of the farmhouses which, since they were so far away from the city centre, were classed as 'low risk'. He was not present at the Management Meeting, or party to the Chief's decision to allow Mr Straw to send Zek and Jack to guard his farmhouse. He did not doubt the boys' courage or good intentions, and he knew from past experience that they were a marvel at scraping through adventures. In fact, these two boys had proved very important to the city of Aletheia. But was it wise to send those so young and inexperienced into the war zone? He looked at the two boys standing earnestly and anxiously in front of his desk, desperate to impress, eager for his confidence. The Bible said if you had faith in God, even faith the size of a mustard seed[7], God could use you. Perhaps, Bourne thought, he should not doubt them, especially in this time of crisis when all willing hands were needed.

"Mr Straw said that the *Chief* said we could do guard duty," reiterated Zek, as politely as he could without being too forceful about the matter.

"You have read our *Guard Duty Rules on Discretion and Discovery?*"

asked Bourne. There were firm rules about guarding all the entry points to underground Aletheia; any indiscretion might lead to their discovery – and that could be catastrophic for a people who wanted to remain hidden and secure until the time was right to take back their city.

Both boys nodded. "We read the Rules *three* times before we came," said Zek, who was always precise. "And we're going to take a copy with us too!"

"That's more than most have read them," muttered Bourne. "And your armour of God…?"[11]

"We've got it all ready," said Zek eagerly. "We've even got extra supplies that Jack brought with him from his home!"

Bourne was interested. Jack's home, in another land altogether, was intriguing to him. Another time, when there wasn't a war pressing on them, perhaps when he was due a holiday, he would like to travel to Jack's world and see it for himself.

After what felt like a long, uncertain pause Bourne said, "Very well, permission granted!"

Zek, forgetting for a moment his dignity and the importance of the mission, let out a squeal of delight which he quickly muffled into a cough. Jack, who was not prone to spontaneous outbursts of any kind, looked sober and responsible.

"Now, you must report back here at the same time tomorrow to tell me how it went. I want a detailed account before we consider further duties!"

"Yes, Bourne…uh, I mean, *sir!*" said Zek.

And, before he could change his mind, the two boys vanished quickly through the door.

Bourne completed the paperwork for the boys' guard duty that night and tapped their whereabouts into his small Mission Detector screen so the boys would show on the large Central Mission Detector screen in the Control Room. That way, at least someone was watching them. He even wondered whether, for once, he should have completed a Risk Assessment.

CHAPTER 13
GUARD DUTY

Jack and Zek's preparations for their guard duty shift did not take long. Everything was ready and they only needed to put on their armour of God[11], and collect Jack's rucksack – and Hector – and they were ready to go. Jack was glad he had come prepared to Aletheia this time. In his rucksack, among his school stuff, was his Bible (which now hung in a pouch from his belt), a water proof jacket, a book borrowed from his father which contained diagrams of some good fighting moves, the small book his teacher had once given him entitled '*Handbook for Adventurous Boys*', and the old boots from the attic which served as his armour of God boots on a previous trip to Aletheia[5] and were the mysterious reason – which his mum couldn't fathom – why his school rucksack weighed so much. The remaining biscuits were rather crumbled since they were jumbled up with the boots, but neither Zek nor Jack nor Hector were too fussy about that.

The boys weren't sure how to find Mr Straw's farmhouse from the underground city. Even if you knew the general direction, things didn't look the same below the ground. They did not like to ask, fearing it might jeopardise their whole mission if they admitted how little they knew. Even Zek had not explored beyond the city centre streets and buildings or followed the quiet, more dimly-lit tunnels which snaked away downwards from the cross and twisted and turned into the unknown. Hector, who *had* explored most of the underground, was frankly not much help. He barked excitedly at every turning, giving them absolutely no clue where he thought they ought to be going, despite Zek's faithful encouragement.

"I don't think Hector can be expected to know *every* tunnel underground," said Zek loyally.

Jack, who was secretly pleased they would *not* be following Hector's directions, agreed. "I expect he knows the streets in the centre the best," he said politely. He wondered what that fierce warrior, Lieutenant Bourne Faithful, might have said about Hector accompanying them on their guard duty. But there was nothing specifically in the *Guard Duty Rules on Discretion and Discovery* that mentioned dogs.

It was eerie walking away from the well-lit, wide, paved streets of the city centre. In the centre of Aletheia the rocky roof of the underground city was tall and remote. The foundations of the buildings stretched high above them until they slipped through the earth into aboveground Aletheia. There was room to breathe in the city centre, but as Jack and Zek walked further away, the rocky roof became lower and lower until they were walking in a tunnel. They took their Bibles out of the pouches at their sides. The warm streetlights of the city centre had ceased and they needed the light of their Bibles[6] to show them the way. They followed underground Pride Way which was signposted from the cross. They knew they needed to turn right off Pride Way and looked anxiously for a tunnel opening.

"Do you think we've come too far?" asked Zek, after they walked some distance.

Jack shrugged. It was impossible to tell how far they had come. "I think it feels further walking underground," he said. "But I think we're under one of the farms now. Look!" He pointed to the ceiling where the roots of a tree protruded through the rock and earth. "It must be a tree on the farmlands!" he said.

Zek searched carefully along the rocky sides of the tunnel as they walked, trying to find an opening or *something* that would lead to Mr Straw's house. "Here!" he said suddenly.

Hector barked loudly in excitement, the noise echoing around them. Jack peered at where Zek was pointing. There was a door fitted into the side of the tunnel, barely visible because it was painted to blend into the walls. A small sign was fixed upon it. It simply said, 'Mr Silage'.

"The way to Mr Silage's farm!" exclaimed Zek. "He's a neighbour of Mr Straw, so we're going the right way, Jack!"

Hector barked loudly again.

"It's a good job we don't need to be quiet," observed Jack, as the ear-splitting sound once more bounced around the walls.

They checked the walls more carefully after that, feeling along them until, at last, they found a sign that read 'Mr Straw'. There was no opening on the door. No way to unfasten it. Instead, in the middle of the door, there was a book-shaped indentation. Both boys knew what this was. It was a Bible-access-only door. Zek pressed his Bible into the indentation and there was a soft *click*. The door opened smoothly before them. They were in another passageway, small, narrow and cramped, and now they were moving in a different direction. Hector did not like it. He barked at the moving light their Bibles cast about them as they walked.

They watched the sides of the tunnel again, wondering if there was another turning they must take. But there was nothing. Instead, the passageway came to a short, undramatic end. There was a sturdy wooden ladder fixed to the wall ahead, which vanished into an open, gaping darkness which was suddenly above them.

There was nothing for it but to climb the ladder into the unknown shadows above. They put Hector – struggling and barking – into Jack's rucksack, and began to climb, Hector protesting loudly all the while.

"Quiet, Hector!" Zek admonished. But the small dog was oblivious to such a rebuke. This was a venture unlike any he had experienced in his short, adventurous life – and he didn't like it at all.

They didn't have to go far. Jack, who led the way, came to an abrupt halt when his head hit a sturdy, wooden trapdoor. "I'm stuck!" he called to Zek below him. "I think it's a door…!"

"Is it Bible-access?" Zek asked anxiously. His voice echoed weirdly around the enclosed shaft. *Bible-access…access…access…*

It was awkward to hold onto the ladder and hold his Bible aloft above him but Jack managed it – although he wished that Hector, now desperate to escape his entrapment in the rucksack, would keep still. He spotted the familiar book-shaped indentation in the wood and placed his Bible firmly in the middle. There was a reassuring *click* and the trapdoor above them swung up on its hinges without any other persuasion. Jack and Zek climbed the last few rungs of the ladder, and scrambled into Mr Straw's farmhouse.

It was strange to be standing in the middle of Mr Straw's once cosy kitchen. Instead of a fire in the old-fashioned stove, and cheery light, and chatter with Mr Straw, there was darkness, and silence, and a distinct chill in the air around them. There was a faint rustle which Jack thought was probably mice. Hector seemed to think so too: once he was released from the rucksack, he gave a joyful yap and dashed through the kitchen door and up the stairs, glad to be free again.

Through the windows, where once there were only reassuring country sounds and stars at night, there was the faint, unsettling flicker of camp fires and the call of strange voices across the Pray-Always Farmlands. Cautiously, Zek and Jack approached the window. Until now they had no real idea of the scale of the invasion of Aletheia. But looking out of the window it felt as if their enemies might be surrounding the farm, awaiting the chance to invade Mr Straw's house, and perhaps even find their way through the trapdoor to underground Aletheia.

After a while, Jack got out his Bible. They thought it best to stay in the dark, but they knew from the *Guard Duty Rules on Discretion and Discovery* that the light of the Bible could never cause them harm, even if it made them known to their enemies. And when Jack held his up to the window, it shone on the dark world beyond, lighting the space with radiant brightness. Suddenly they could clearly see the garden, and the trees, and the barn.

But then they spotted the barn door. It was not locked and fastened as they knew it should be.

It was ajar.

And open to the invaders of Aletheia!

CHAPTER 14
SECURITY BREACH!

The two boys looked in dismay at the open barn door. Everything should be locked up tight! If there was an entry point to underground Aletheia in the barn, this was surely a breach in the security of the whole underground city!

"We don't know for sure that there is an underground entry from the barn," remarked Jack.

"But what if there *is*?" said Zek. "We have to secure it!"

Jack, who usually did not like rules and regulations, tried to remember what the *Guard Duty Rules on Discretion and Discovery* said about such an eventuality. "There *were* exceptions to the rules," he said slowly.

"Exactly!" said Zek. "I'm sure there was one about going outside when there was *imminent danger to safety* – or something like that."

Jack wasn't certain what 'imminent danger' meant under the circumstances; with all the invaders about, Aletheia was in imminent danger anyway. He wondered if there was anything in his *Handbook for Adventurous Boys* which explained what 'imminent danger' was – but, when they checked, there was only something quite pointless about good citizens always dialling 999 if there was "real and imminent danger to life". Jack didn't think that was very useful advice for the situation they faced, and Zek couldn't understand it at all. He had never heard of dialling 999 in Aletheia!

"I guess we'll have to go and secure the barn door," Jack said slowly.

"Yes," agreed Zek, "it's up to us!"

They didn't discuss it further. Zek just said, "I expect it's best to leave Hector in the house." And Jack, realising what a disruptive influence Hector would be when they were trying to remain discreet and undiscovered, agreed. In any case, Hector, judging by faint, muffled, joyful yaps, would not miss them at all. There appeared to be plenty to occupy Hector in Mr Straw's deserted farmhouse.

All was quiet outside. The water-wheel, which usually powered the house, was still and silent. The stream over which the house was built, which was once the pure Water of Sound Doctrine, trickled by slowly and sadly, as if it knew it was unwell, polluted by the Meddlers' poison. Mr Straw's vegetable garden still contained a few potatoes and carrots poking through the soil; the apple and plum trees in the orchard near the house were hanging with spoiling fruit, but at least they were still standing. But further away from the house, Jack and Zek were horrified to see fruit trees cut down, the branches strewn over the once neat pasture, and the fruit trampled roughly underfoot by the feet of invaders who didn't care about the Pray-Always Farmlands at all.

The two boys ventured further from the house, creeping down the path to the big farm shed where they had held their meetings last spring, when they were the Mustardseeds[3]. They both put away their Bibles; darkness seemed the best cover. But it was hard walking. The ground was sticky and gooey, as if it was trying to make them stick and stumble.

"Stumbles," whispered Zek. "Stumbles have invaded Aletheia!"

Jack had never seen a Stumble before but it was not hard to imagine them. They were earth-bound creatures, cleverly camouflaged and almost impossible to see except with the light of the Bible. They were extremely sticky and used hundreds of tiny grabbers, which were like sticky labels, to clutch the feet of anything that trod on them. It was almost impossible to walk over them for any distance except with armour of God[11] boots. Jack and Zek were both wearing their armour boots, but it was still hard work walking across a path of sticky Stumbles.

Around them, at the fringes of the farm, they knew there were shadows watching them too. The Snares of the land of Err had followed the invaders to Aletheia and now they surrounded Mr Straw's farm. The evil glitter of their eyes was fixed on the two boys and Zek clutched

Jack's arm. They had met Snares on a previous adventure[2], and, while they were frightening creatures, they knew how to defeat them. Both boys quickly reached for the Bibles which were secure in pouches at their sides. Jack was certain he heard the disappointed hisses of the Snares who feared the light of the Word of God and could not come closer. And the clouds of Sloths floating lazily above, drifted to a nearby camp of invaders where they were more welcome.

Warm, bright, wonderfully reassuring light spilled from the pages of the Bibles. Suddenly the Stumbles which clutched at their feet retreated with weird, disgruntled, squeaking sounds as they fled from the path before the boys. At last their way seemed clear as light spilled around them. They didn't care that all the foes and creatures which had invaded Aletheia might see. They remembered once more that the light of the Word of God would never cause them harm.

When they reached the open barn door, Jack clutched his Bible more tightly in his hand and led the way on silent feet. Zek was happy to let Jack take the lead. He had great confidence in Jack's ability to deal with difficult or uncertain situations. It was one of the things that made Jack such a great companion on adventures.

They ventured through the door into the dark interior of the barn. At first it seemed they were alone. There were no animals in the barn, of course; they were safely underground. There might have been a few small creatures, sheltering from the cold, damp autumn night. But, as the Bible shone into the dark corners of the empty barn, on the few remaining bales of straw and piles of hay, the rays of light showed a very strange sight.

Dusty Addle rubbed his eyes sleepily, startled awake by the distinct warning bleep from the huge Central Mission Detector screen in the Control Room of the Academy. In these anxious times there was always someone on duty in the Control Room. They were allowed to nap on night duty, and most of the staff learned to sleep with one ear open for any alarm from the complex machines in the Control Room.

Dusty made his way quickly to the huge Mission Detector screen, instantly spotting the orange flashing light which indicated a 'Security Breach'. It wasn't the bright red which indicated a serious breach and imminent danger, but, nonetheless, the light meant that underground Aletheia might be at risk and it must be investigated. Oddly enough, it was coming from a farmhouse on Pray-Always Farmlands. That was strange because, as far as Dusty knew, they didn't have enough guards to cover the farmhouses for regular guard duty. They were on the rota for 'spot checks' only. Dusty rapidly pressed keys on a small screen beneath the massive Mission Detector. Within the blink of an eye, the device showed the following message:

'Security Breach: Location: Farmhouse – Straw; Guard Duty: approved by Lieutenant Faithful; Guards: Hezekiah Amos Wallop, Jack Arnold Merryweather…'

"Well, I never!" exclaimed Dusty to himself. "Jack and Zek in the thick of things again!" He pondered the decision he must now take. He had a great deal of confidence in the two boys and was not anxious to bring the wrath of hardworking Lieutenant Faithful down on their heads at this hour of the night. He would observe a little longer and see what should be done. He watched the massive screen where two green dots, which he knew were Jack and Zek, moved from the farmhouse – which he now knew was Mr Straw's – towards one of the farm buildings close by.

"The old barn," mused Dusty, who never minded speaking to himself. "Our old meeting place when we were the Mustardseeds! I wonder what they can want there…!"

Whatever they were up to, and despite the fact Dusty loved his

Control Room duties, he wished he was back at the old barn with them. But, since he wasn't there and could not assist them with his presence, Dusty began to pray.

CHAPTER 15
WONKY DOLLAR

Jack and Zek stared at the tatty, unkempt man seated at the back of the barn. He was lit by a faint, flickering lamp which was decidedly unfriendly next to the bright, strong light of the Bible. The man clearly made his bed in the soft hay and was blinking uncertainly at the two boys whom he could barely see behind the blinding light suddenly shining upon him.

"W-Who is it?" asked the man.

"Who are you?" asked Jack, moving closer. Whatever, and whoever, the man was, he didn't seem like a threat.

"W-Wonky Dollar, a-a-at your service," stammered the man.

"Mr Dollar!" exclaimed Jack in disbelief.

"Wonky Dollar!" exclaimed Zek, equally surprised.

The last time they had seen Mr Wonky Dollar he was full of confidence because Jack had inadvertently helped him to make a lot of money[2]: and Wonky Dollar loved money. But now…how had poor Wonky Dollar been reduced to this scruffy man who was trying to find shelter from the cold night air?

"Are you-are you…" It seemed Mr Dollar recognised Jack too, and he got to his feet in excitement, clasping Jack by the hand. "The Lego

Treasure boy[2]! My luck has changed at last!" he exclaimed. "My dear boy! However did you find me?"

"Uh…" Jack was stunned almost to silence. He had never tried to bring Wonky Dollar 'luck', and he hadn't set out to find him. In actual fact, Jack always felt sorry he was never able to help Mr Dollar in the way he most needed. He had never managed to direct him to the cross where he could have his sins forgiven because of the Lord Jesus[12], and find the contentment that money could never bring. And now Wonky Dollar was in Aletheia when things were at their worst! How could they help him now?

"We weren't trying to find you," said Zek, who was always literal and frank. "We were checking on the farmlands. What are you doing in Mr Straw's shed?"

Wonky Dollar watched the boys with interest. "You *can* help me," he said, as though he was speaking to himself. "You're the very ones to show me the way!"

"The way to the cross?" asked Jack.

"The cross?" echoed Wonky Dollar. "I don't know about that! I saw plenty of gold crosses on my way here, but they didn't seem to do me much good at all! I gave them the last of my money, and they told me all my sins[15] are forgiven and that God will bless me with riches. But I haven't made any money yet and I still don't know how! No, not the cross. It's the *competition* I want to win!"

"Competition?" asked Zek. "We're nothing to do with a competition!"

"You can't pay money to have your sins forgiven!" said Jack.

"But you'll know the answers, you see?" said Mr Dollar earnestly.

"No, I don't think so," said Zek. "I'm never very good at quizzes and competitions in school. I never know enough of the answers to the questions!"

"What happened to the rest of your money?" asked Jack, still wondering how Wonky Dollar came to be in this sad state.

"Gone," said Wonky gloomily. "All gone. The last of it went to the folk on The Outskirts who promised me that if I gave it to their gold-cross church I would get back even more than I gave! But that didn't work at all!"

"Did the rest of it fly away?" asked Jack.

"Most of it did," said Wonky. "That's what it always does, doesn't it? Money always flies away![13]"

Jack didn't bother to explain to Wonky Dollar that money only flew away when you loved it too much. He didn't think Wonky Dollar would ever understand.

"But now, see about this competition..." Wonky Dollar continued eagerly.

"What competition?" asked Zek. "We're really not very good at them, you know."

"The Reform Aletheia Competition!" said Wonky Dollar. "You must know about it, since you seem to, uh, know about Aletheia, you see?" His eyes took on a decidedly cunning twinkle. "Are you-are you boys *Aletheians?*" he asked.

"Of course we are!" said Zek.

Jack's sharp nudge in his ribs was too late. Zek suddenly looked crestfallen and very uncertain. Wonky Dollar noticed the boys' sudden concern and nodded comfortingly. "It's alright," he said reassuringly. "We don't want to cause you any harm, it's all to *help* the Aletheians, you see."

"To help us?" squeaked Zek incredulously, understanding at last that the competition to which Wonky Dollar referred was connected to the land of Err. Through the barn door the campfires flickered ominously on the Pray-Always Farmlands, burning the fragrant branches of the orchards of Aletheia. If this was the assistance of Err, the competition was a very bad joke!

Wonky Dollar took Zek's question seriously, as if he could alleviate his fears. "I think the Council of Err are worried because the people, uh, disappeared," he said.

"I bet they're worried," said Jack sarcastically.

"The competition is to help them locate the people," said Wonky. "Do *you* know where they are?"

"I suppose there's money for winning the competition," remarked Jack perceptively, ignoring the question.

"Well, as a matter of fact, I was going to mention that I'm happy to share some of m-my winnings…"

"Share?!" echoed Zek, too outraged to express how he felt about this awful competition and the thought of betraying Aletheia for money.

"Yes, share it," said Wonky Dollar, puzzled at, but not comprehending, the boys' reaction. "It's, uh, one hundred Erona…" He hoped the boys didn't know how much the prize money was; he was anxious for their assistance, but not anxious to share *all* the winnings and he didn't think a tiny lie would hurt them.

Jack wondered why Wonky Dollar was suddenly shifting uneasily. "I think you'll find the answers you need at the cross," he said. "Not the gold cross where they took your money, but at the cross in the centre of Aletheia, the one which represents where the Lord Jesus died."[12]

"That's it, Jack!" exclaimed Zek. "*That's* the right answer! I knew you'd think of it!"

Wonky Dollar was bemused. "But that's not the answer *I'm* looking for," he said. "I don't think that's the right answer at all!"

Jack rummaged in his rucksack. There was nothing else he could think to do for Wonky Dollar but to share the supply of biscuits in his rucksack and persuade him to leave the barn so they could make it secure. Mr Dollar thanked him politely but he was looking rather oddly at the boys. As Jack saw him in the light of the Bible, he had an uneasy feeling Mr Dollar was not going to accept their answers.

And now they had a real problem.

Suppose Wonky Dollar followed them to the farmhouse and saw the trapdoor in the kitchen? Mr Dollar could betray the city for money! Surprisingly, Wonky Dollar left the barn without any protest, but Jack was very anxious as he and Zek watched him walk away with his bundle to one of the camps on the Pray-Always Farmlands. Then they put away their Bibles, fearing Wonky Dollar might follow the light. They crept back through the shadows across the Stumbles to the farmhouse. Once or twice the boys looked over their shoulders. Was there a shadow, perhaps a random Snare, following them…?

They reached the farmhouse door, and, as Jack was hesitating, wondering whether they were leading Mr Dollar straight into underground Aletheia, there was the most terrific commotion! There was a cry from the corner of the house, and then a loud splash as a figure, who could only be Wonky Dollar, fell headlong into the stream of the polluted Water of Sound Doctrine. The quiet night was shattered by his howl and by fierce, outraged barking on the banks of the stream. And there was Fly, the collie, her teeth bared in a vicious grin.

"Fly!" cried Jack with joy.

Fly dashed through the stream and leapt at both boys, covering them in exuberant, affectionate licks. Then she dashed back again to stand guard at the bank of the stream, snarling angrily at the poor, shabby, soaked and forlorn figure, who evidently did not dare to extract himself from the shallow water.

"H-h-help!" cried Wonky Dollar. "H-help!"

"You were following us!" said Zek, almost as outraged as Fly.

"I only wanted to see where you were going!" wailed Wonky Dollar. "Take this wild dog away! Please take her away!"

"She doesn't like betrayers of Aletheia," said Zek darkly. The reference was lost on Wonky Dollar, who had no idea of betraying Aletheia, only of winning money. And it was just as well for him that

Fly didn't know how to distinguish a 'betrayer of Aletheia' from any of the other invaders of the farmlands. She treated them all with equal disdain.

Jack ignored the altercation between Zek and Mr Dollar and examined Fly who once more joyfully returned to him. She was sleek, and gleaming, and having the time of her life. She had clearly eaten enough, and was now catching Meddlers and annoying the nearby campsites by pinching their food and disrupting their picnics. She fiercely guarded Mr Straw's domain and was largely responsible for the fact that his house, garden, and orchard were not touched by the invaders. And she guarded the entry to underground Aletheia as if her life depended on it. There was no need for any other guard here!

"I think you should get away from Mr Straw's farm," Zek was saying sternly to Mr Dollar. "And don't ever come back, or next time Fly will eat you!"

"I only want to win the competition," said Mr Dollar, scrambling out of the stream on the further side, while Jack held onto Fly who had, sometime during her adventures of the past few weeks, lost her collar. Wonky Dollar grabbed his scruffy bundle, and, with Zek looking indignantly after him, vanished towards the nearest campfire.

"Remember the cross," called Jack. "Look for answers at the cross!"

Dusty's attention never wavered from the two green dots on the huge Mission Detector screen. They represented Jack and Zek, and Dusty watched until they returned to the safety of the farmhouse. The orange security breach light blinked off and the incident was over.

Dusty could detect none of the details. But, "I'll have to file a report for Lieutenant Faithful," he said to himself. "If I put it in his afternoon post tomorrow, it will give the boys a chance to explain…"

He returned to slumber.

His prayers for their safety had been heard.

CHAPTER 16
THE DEBRIEF

Jack had some misgivings about their upcoming debrief with Lieutenant Bourne Faithful the afternoon following their guard duty. Zek was unfailingly optimistic that, by leaving the farmhouse, they had taken the only reasonable course of action they could. In fact, by Zek's way of thinking, the two boys might have single-handedly saved Aletheia on their very first guard duty! But even Zek was nervous when he stood in front of his cousin, who was now his commanding officer, catching his fierce frown as they relayed their experiences of the previous night. Once or twice Bourne put his hand over his face; once or twice he sighed.

"There is *no* underground entry in the barns of Aletheia," he said. "The open barn door did *not* constitute *imminent danger* to underground Aletheia."

"But it might have done," said Zek earnestly. "Don't you see, Bour-sir, that we didn't know about that bit, and so we thought the open door *might* have meant *imminent danger* to Aletheia!"

"I can see your reasoning, certainly," said Bourne drily.

"We did remember rules in the *Guard Duty Rules on Discretion and Discovery*, and there was nothing that said we *shouldn't go...*"

Zek was anxious to explain.

Bourne groaned faintly.

"And we even checked Jack's Handbook!"

"What Handbook?" Bourne asked curiously.

"Well, it didn't exactly apply to the situation," said Jack cautiously. He knew, even if Zek did not, that his *Handbook for Adventurous Boys* would not help their case with Lieutenant Faithful. "How did the animals get underground, sir?" Jack asked politely, changing the subject. "I thought there must be an underground entry point for the animals, from the barns."

Bourne was slightly more impressed. There was no doubt Jack Merryweather was a smart boy and a quick thinker. Perhaps that was why he sailed through his various adventures. "I can see how you might think that," he said.

"Yes, that's right, Jack!" Zek piped up. "Good thinking!" He trailed off when he once more met the steely glance of his oldest cousin. Bourne was not impressed with them.

"The Academy of Soldiers-of-the-Cross contains the main entry point for animals and goods," Bourne explained briefly.

Jack imagined all the animals being driven through the streets of Aletheia, into the Academy. Cows mooing as they walked through the echoing, marble corridors…

What other mysteries did the vast fortress hold?

"Did you even consider prayer cover for your aboveground excursion?" asked Bourne.

Both boys shook their heads dolefully. There were so many things to think about on a mission. How could they possibly remember them all on their very first guard duty?

"We did get rid of Wonky Dollar though," said Zek anxiously. "We really did, Bour-sir!"

"Zek told Wonky Dollar that Fly would eat him if he came back," said Jack, thinking to help their cause. He wasn't sure it did exactly help. But it looked, for a moment, as if Bourne was on the verge of smiling. "I told him to go to the cross," added Jack.

"Did you?" asked Bourne, and his frown lifted at last.

At that moment Henrietta Wallop, dressed in the smart uniform of the staff of the Academy, appeared with the afternoon reports in her hand. "Your afternoon post, sir!" she said cheerfully. She looked interestedly at the two young visitors to Bourne's office, standing meekly before his desk. Since she had been speaking to Dusty, and his was one of the reports in her hand, she knew very well why Jack and Zek were there.

"You really should learn to knock, Henry," remarked Bourne.

"Uh, right, sir," said Henrietta, still very cheerful. And she saluted smartly.

Zek giggled, and then coughed and spluttered, mortified he had almost laughed in the face of his severe commanding officer who was already distinctly displeased with them.

"You may go, Henry," Bourne said drily. He shook his head. But, although the kids were providing him with some trying moments amongst all his other duties, he was secretly amused at them too. His cousin Henrietta's current duties, which were basically to be his dogsbody and to fetch and carry and be at his beck and call, were intended to be a punishment for the apple core throwing incident when she was on guard duty at the Judges' Academy. But Henry didn't view it as a punishment at all. Although she wasn't able to go aboveground and take guard duty shifts until Bourne decided otherwise, she still felt she was in the thick of the action at Bourne's right hand. She had even requested to stay as his 'assistant'! Bourne hadn't made any comment about that, but he was forced to admit she was proving remarkably efficient and useful.

Bourne quickly leafed through the reports Henrietta handed him, his practiced eye immediately spotting the Security Breach. The boys stood still and watchful as Bourne read the report. They didn't know what it was. They had no idea that their leaving Mr Straw's farmhouse had been noted in the Control Room. But Bourne had been expecting the report. If the two boys had left the safety of the Bible-access-only farmhouse, the Central Mission Detector should have spotted it, and the hardworking Dusty would have been the one to record the findings.

"Dusty Addle has filed a report about your Security Breach," he said to the boys. They still weren't sure what this entailed and kept silent. "I think you have Dusty to thank for the fact this didn't reach my desk before you did," Bourne added perceptively.

"Good for Dusty!" whispered Zek to Jack, still puzzled what their friend knew of their escapade.

"Could Dusty see us from the Control Room?" asked Jack. He had never visited that auspicious place.

"He could track your movements," said Bourne.

"And he knew it was us?" said Jack with awe.

Bourne nodded. "I entered you into the system when you went on guard duty." He glanced back at the report. "But there's something else you should know," he said. And Jack and Zek held their breath, fearing that they had committed another misdemeanour. Did Hector, chasing mice and barking at full volume, show up on the Mission Detector too? "When you were at risk, outside of the farmhouse, Dusty was praying for you. So you did have prayer cover after all."

Zek exhaled with relief.

"I believe Dusty included that in his report to spare you any unpleasant repercussions," observed Bourne. His tone was dry, but the twinkle in his eye was discernible enough. He no longer seemed so displeased. "You are dismissed," he added to the two boys.

And, with considerable relief, they fled the room.

CHAPTER 17
THE FOOD DISTRIBUTION CENTRE

Benjamin Wright lived with his parents and younger brother and sister in underground Aletheia. He was a talkative boy with a perpetual grin and countless freckles, and by nature he was cheerful, funny and likeable. At school he was the bane of his Headmaster, Mr Mustardpot's, life and was usually in trouble with one prank or another.

Benjamin was very pleased when school was shut and all the adults became busy focussing on the aboveground invasion. His father, Sturdy Wright, was a very important man in Aletheia. He was the Head Keeper of the Water of Sound Doctrine, and all of Benjamin's friends and cousins, like Hugo and Henrietta Wallop and Josie Faithful, were doing important and exciting things for the defence of the city.

Benjamin wanted to do his bit for Aletheia just like everyone else, but the war had become rather unsatisfactory. Instead of action, he was stuck with the oldies in the Food Distribution Centre, counting fruit and vegetables and making up ration boxes for the people of the underground city. "Not a bean must be lost!" was Mr Mustardpot's favourite saying when he patrolled the Food Distribution Centre, helping his friend, Croft Straw, oversee the food rationing. The old folk, who were the bulk of the workforce, enjoyed Mr Mustardpot's uplifting visits, but Benjamin didn't care much for beans; frankly, he didn't think it would matter if they were all lost. Nor was Mr Philologus Mustardpot Benjamin's favourite person. Mr Mustardpot had volunteered Benjamin to work at the underground Food Distribution Centre, the only young person amongst a sea of old people who were volunteers from Run-the-Race Retirement Home.

Of course, Benjamin knew why he couldn't do something more exciting like guard duty aboveground. It was because his Bible didn't work. It never had. It was the same Bible everyone else had, but it didn't show light. Benjamin thought that everything in the Bible was probably true, but the adults said that his Bible didn't show light because he didn't have trust and confidence in it[16]. After a while he stopped using it.

Benjamin placed another four apples in the apple compartment of yet another neat cardboard box. He pushed it down the long table to his new and interesting neighbour, the old man who stood next to him on the Pray-Always food assembly line. The old man scrutinised his list, solemnly placed two pears in the box, and passed it on. An old lady was assigned to plums, then the box passed to the 'vegetables' section of the assembly line where potatoes, carrots, leeks, beetroot, beans and all sorts of other vegetables were added, each person checking their list so that exactly the right amount was added according to each Aletheian family's requirements and preferences.

Benjamin's neighbour was new to the Food Distribution Centre. He was an exceedingly odd man who tried painstakingly hard to get everything exactly right. He didn't talk much to Benjamin as they worked – because he couldn't count pears for the food boxes and talk at the same time. But when they stopped for their morning break, at which they were allowed to eat one item of fruit of their choice, Benjamin took his chance. He chose a plum to eat (he was fed up with apples), and sat on a wooden pallet by the old man. The old man was wearing clothes that were all the wrong size, as if they were borrowed from lots of different people, none of whom were the same size as him. And he wore the most enormous glasses, through which his eyes were magnified in the most extraordinary way. He brought his old, battered Bible to work as if he couldn't bear to let it go. It wasn't necessary to carry a Bible everywhere in underground Aletheia, but this man kept his by his hand, where it was always within reach.

Even in times of boredom and frustration, Benjamin tended to make the most of the situation and this old man was definitely interesting. If his best friend, Charlie Steady, hadn't been sent away for the war, they could have had some fun here.

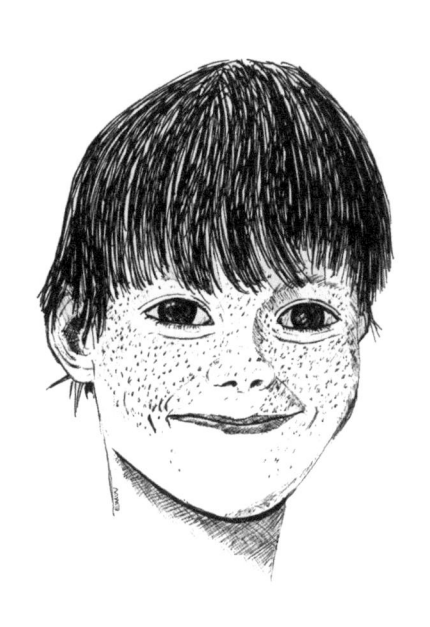

"Are you a refugee?" Benjamin asked the old man curiously. There were many newcomers to underground Aletheia these days, mostly coming from The Outskirts.

"R-refugee?" The old man was puzzled so Benjamin didn't pursue it.

"Do you have bad eyesight?" he asked next, fixing on the huge glasses.

"Are they testing eyes for the war effort?" asked the old man. "I can assure you I'm more than able to do my food distribution duties! They won't make me give up my duties, will they?"

Benjamin didn't have any idea about that, but he felt sorry for the strange old man. "Oh, I shouldn't think so," he said kindly. "They need everyone to do something, don't they? And pears are big enough to see, aren't they? I mean, it's not like counting tiny peas!"

The old man nodded soberly. "It's very good of a youngster like you to be helping here," he said earnestly.

Benjamin felt guilty at how begrudging his help was.

"I'm not used to sitting around either," confided the old man. "I'm more of a man of action, like you are, I'm sure."

Benjamin looked at him curiously. "What's your name?" he asked.

"My name? Dim View at your service, young sir!"

Benjamin roared with sudden infectious laughter, startling several old people who were glad to take a quiet break from the labours of the day. "Dim View! Ha! Ha! Ha!" he chuckled. Then he came to an abrupt halt. He didn't mean to be rude; he was just struck at the great joke of a man called Dim View with those massive, all-seeing glasses. "It was the glasses," he began to explain earnestly.

"My g-g-glasses?" quavered Dim View, rather puzzled. "They got me new glasses from the store," he said. "I don't need my spy goggles anymore, you see?"

"Spy goggles?!" exclaimed Benjamin. "Have you actually been a *spy* in a war?"

The old man drew closer. "I considered myself in the secret-hidden-service," he confided. "Spying, watching, waiting…"

"Did you?" asked Benjamin, greatly intrigued. "I didn't know the Academy of Soldiers-of-the-Cross had a secret service! I wonder if I could…"

"No, not the Academy!" Dim View shook his head sadly. "I was mistaken. We, at No-Witness Apartments, were wrong. Iniquity abounds, wars and rumours of wars, but the cross of the Lord Jesus will be ever victorious! There is no need to hide and spy!"

"Oh," said Benjamin, disappointed there might not be, after all, a thrilling secret service at the Academy. "But you *are* a refugee from The Outskirts?"

"We returned to the cross!" said Dim View emphatically. "And we're never moving away from the cross again!"

"The war won't last forever, you know," said Benjamin wisely. He knew there were plans afoot to retake the city. He didn't know what the plans were, but he always had confidence that the might of the Academy of Soldiers-of-the-Cross would win the day.

"We came back to the cross of the Lord Jesus," continued Dim View. "At the cross, everything is based on Justification!"[14]

"Uh, right," said Benjamin.

"It's how the war can be won!"

"Is it?" asked Benjamin, wondering how batty the old man was. "Have you told the folks at the Academy your ideas?"

"They know it too," said Dim View. "Look for the answers in Justification."

"There's a place called Justification in Aletheia," said Benjamin politely.

"You can't pay gold to have your sins forgiven," said the old man.

"Is that what they're saying?" asked Benjamin. He knew very little about the new message being introduced on The Outskirts of Aletheia. But he knew that wasn't what Aletheia taught. From a child he had learned that the only way to have your sins forgiven was through the Lord Jesus.

"Dreadful iniquity!" said Dim View. "Only the blood of the Lord Jesus can pay the debt we owe! It's about Justification, you see! No amount of gold in the world can pay for sin! The payment is in blood!"

Benjamin was getting restless. Secretly, he didn't understand why gold crosses and whatever message was sneaking into Aletheia was such a big deal. He deplored the invasion of the city; but people could believe what they wanted, couldn't they?

After his shift at the Food Distribution Centre, Benjamin bumped into his cousin, Zek Wallop, and Zek's friend, Jack Merryweather. He was very pleased to meet Jack, of whose adventures he had heard. Those adventures were exactly the type that appealed to Benjamin. And when he heard they had been aboveground on the Pray-Always Farmlands, in on the war action, Benjamin's admiration – and envy – knew no bounds.

"I wish they would let me do guard duty," he said.

"Why can't you?" asked Jack.

Benjamin shrugged. He was always uncomfortable with the reason. "My Bible doesn't work,"[16] he said. "I've given up on it."

"The Bible *always* works," said Jack, "for *everyone!*"

"Benjamin doesn't believe in it," said Zek. "That's why he doesn't see the light."

"That's *not* why!" said Benjamin. He didn't like to talk about it. He wished his friend, Charlie Steady, was with him; Charlie's Bible wasn't light to him either.

"It's because you haven't trusted in the Lord Jesus for yourself and become a Christian,"[1] said Zek. It was a well-known fact. So well known they had all got used to it. Benjamin shrugged again. He felt alright. And he didn't want to talk about it further. "Can you ask if I can go with you to do guard duty on the farmlands sometime?" he asked hopefully.

"We're not allowed to go back to the farmlands," said Jack ruefully.

"Bad luck!" said Benjamin.

"We're going to join the guards at Justification, though," said Zek. "It's a very important assignment."

Benjamin thought how strange it was that Justification was mentioned by Dim View and now by Jack and Zek too. He remembered the large, stone building on one of the sides of Redemption Square. It was big and solid with huge pillars that were impressive enough. But it wasn't a particularly interesting place.

Why was Justification so important?

CHAPTER 18
THE COUNCIL OF ERR

The Council of Err was assembled. Fourteen people, representatives of fourteen Regions of Err, sat around a large table in the palatial Government building which was situated in a leafy park, not far from the towns of Genius and Deceiverton in Region 2, in the south of the land of Err. Only Region 15 was absent from the gathering. 'Region 15' was the name Err gave to the prosperous city of Aletheia. Nothing, not great promises, bribery, threats, bullying, and, at last, open invasion and warfare, had persuaded Region 15 to join with the Council of Err. The city of Aletheia would not join with Err; they would not deny the Truth they held so dear.

This meeting was unlike any other which had ever taken place in the auspicious headquarters of the Council of Err. Usually the far flung Regions of Err were cajoled or threatened into attending a Government meeting. The meetings were, on the whole, quite pointless – most of the Regions were well aware that Region 2 manipulated and overruled the others. They resented it, but they were usually quieted by bribery and glad to be saved the inconvenience of Government matters. But this time the meeting was called by the various representatives of the Regions. For the first time ever they demanded the Governor answer their complaints about Region 15 – that mysterious city of Aletheia.

Governor Genie quietly seethed with anger as the thirteen other Regions present at the meeting made loud claims on the treasure of the city of Aletheia that they were sure had now been recovered. The Governor had been too eager to impress the other Regions with the story of the victory over the stubborn city in the centre of the land. The Government had quickly announced the complete overthrow of the city: and then promptly discovered the impenetrable buildings of the city withstood their greatest efforts. In addition, there was the complete disappearance of the people of Aletheia! How could the Governor explain they were unable to even touch the stones of the fortress Academy of Soldiers-of-the-Cross – which most of Err were convinced contained great wealth and treasures?

"The flag of the cross still flies from the fortress," growled the fierce and generally avoided representative from Region 10, a man from the terrifying Mountains of Destruction in the north of the land. "Why have our forces been unable to enter the stronghold of the city?"

"This is precisely what we have our best team of scientists and academics researching as we speak," said the Governor smoothly, using her most diplomatic tone. She didn't want to mention the strange sensation that anyone who even touched the building experienced. It was a bit like an electric shock!

"Scientists and academics!" scoffed the man from the Mountains of Destruction. "What we need at this point are bulldozers and fighters!"

"What about the rumour of a *missile* thrown from the Judges' Academy?" asked the generally dozy woman from the town of Dreamy in Region 4. She was seated in an armchair which contained dozens of plump, downy cushions and she perpetually gave the impression of being in a trance. "Do you think the missile is perhaps, uh, a coded message from the, uh, Alien Beings which might be inhabiting the buildings?" asked Dreamy.

"No, I don't," said Governor Genie shortly, trying to keep her temper. The odd thing was, the missile was an *apple core*; it looked suspiciously like a childish prank! The scientists from the Academy of Science-Explains-All carefully analysed the apple core which came from the impenetrable darkness of the Judges' Academy. They were *still* testing it. But so far they had discovered nothing but that it was, indeed, a regular apple core, remarkably free of any pollutants from the land of Err.

"We would like *first* knowledge of the discovery of the Alien Beings we are certain are behind this strange, invisible defence of the buildings," said the representative from Region 13, a man from the town of Make-Believe.

"Well, what a surprise!" scoffed the man from Mockton sarcastically. "I don't see why you should be the first to know!" snapped the woman from the town of Resentment.

"We have no evidence of actual *alien* beings residing in the city," said the Governor. It was nothing new that someone from the town of Make-Believe should hold weird theories about the inhabitants of Aletheia. "But I assure you, if we uncover evidence of…well, of an entirely different species of being, we will inform you at once and you may take whatever steps you need to, uh, analyse the, uh, species!" It was hard to take the representative of Region 13 seriously and Governor Genie utterly despised the silliness of the man. He attended the meeting dressed as a donkey, complete with a donkey head. Through the head of the donkey the small, beady eyes of a man gleamed weirdly. It didn't help that the representative from Mockton kept braying '*hee-haw*' whenever the 'donkey' had anything to say.

Governor Genie knew very well that there was nothing *alien* about the people who used to inhabit Aletheia, wherever they now were. She had once met the Chief of the city, a man who was remarkably intelligent and sane, particularly when compared to the regional representatives by whom she was now surrounded.

"We *insist* on *assisting* with the inventory of the treasure which is undoubtedly hidden in the fortress Region 15 call the Academy of Soldiers-of-the-Cross," said the representative of Region 6, a pompous man from Know-It-All, whose Region also included the town of Love-Of-Riches.

"You have my word that everything will be fairly accounted for," said the Governor smoothly. She didn't mean it, of course. And nobody in their right mind ever trusted the word of the representative of Region 2, even if she was the elected Governor.

"We'll be following progress closely," threatened Know-It-All.

Governor Genie ignored Know-It-All. She already knew that the more astute Regions had people wandering the streets of Aletheia, spying and reporting everything they found.

"We don't want anyone hurt in Aletheia," murmured the representative from the town of Tragedy. "They're very kind to us!"

The representative from Region 14, from the town of Drink-n-Drugs-Upon-Hollow, snored softly from a low beanbag which was almost beneath the table. She had demanded early intelligence of any interesting substances found in Region 15, and then, her job done, promptly fell asleep.

"What about the Reform Aletheia Competition?" asked the more intelligent representative from Region 3, who was from the town of White-Lie.

"The competition is certainly spurring people on to search for the disappeared people of the city," said the Governor, glad for at least one intelligent contributor, although she was very wary of the clever scrutiny of Region 3. Probably Region 3 had their people spying all over Aletheia.

"I don't think this Reform Aletheia Competition will work," said a man from the town of Doubt in Region 12.

"So, when this fails, what, if anything, is the plan, Governor?" sneered Mockton. "Or has Region 2 at last run out of ideas?"

"Region 2 has never let us down in the past!" said White-Lie, which wasn't remotely true.

"There are a number of options, I'm sure," suggested a woman from the town of Compromise.

"I'm not sure there's anything that *can* be done," said Doubt.

"The answer might come to us in a vision," murmured Dreamy.

"It's all to do with aliens from other planets," said Make-Believe.

"Crush the city!" thundered Destruction.

"I don't see why they should be left in peace!" muttered Resentment peevishly.

"But don't bury all the treasure in the rubble!" warned Know-It-All.

Governor Genie held her peace. She knew what they would do next.

They were largely untried and untested by the Academy of Science-Explains-All:

But it was time to release the Deceivedors.

CHAPTER 19
THE DECEIVEDORS

"Jack?" Harris Merryweather peered through the crack in the door through which his brother had vanished. He had heard Jack scraping and pushing through the narrow pipe beyond the door, but now there was silence. "Did we find Aletheia, Jack?" he called. He sat back on his heels and considered what to do. Jack had only been gone a minute or two and he knew he should be patient. But it wouldn't hurt to wait inside the intriguing wooden door, and Harris decided to do exactly that. It was more of an adventure than waiting in the soggy ditch, especially since it was starting to rain.

Harris was smaller than Jack and he squeezed quite easily through the crack in the door. He found the pipe easier to navigate than Jack had done too, even with his school rucksack on his back. He crawled over the moist dirt and dried leaves down the tiny tunnel. Like Jack, he was not too concerned about how to reverse the journey. If his brother came this way, then it must be alright. Harris reached the bend in the pipe, and suddenly, most unexpectedly, everything changed.

He crawled through the entry to the very large cavern: and stopped in horror. In front of him was the strangest gathering he could ever imagine. Instinctively, Harris knew it was not a meeting where he would be welcome, and he ducked behind a nearby rock and peeped cautiously at the fantastic scene.

It was like being trapped in a horrible dream. The cavern was lit with a few flickering lanterns which cast strange, weirdly moving shadows on the walls. Around the massive cave, in some semblance of order, were seated ugly, bulbous creatures which were unlike anything Harris had ever seen before. They had heads, and bodies, and arms, and legs, as people did; and eyes, and ears, and noses, and mouths, all in approximately the right place; but their bodies were distorted, as if all the parts weren't exactly sure how big they were meant to be, and what shape was intended either. They were clothed in tatty, disgusting garments that didn't fit. It was almost as if they were unfinished mutations that someone had discarded too early in their creation. They were speaking together, and Harris could understand their words which were formed through a curious hissing sound. It was – it was just as you might imagine a snake to speak. It was a very peculiar accent.

In the centre of the cavern, clearly in charge, was a particularly massive brute that was enormously fat and clothed in a bizarre blue robe which might have been intended to portray dignity and importance. But now the gold fringe was dirty and frayed, and there was an inconvenient hole in the body of the robe with which the wretch fiddled as he talked.

"Thes Masterss ares honourings uss withs thiss specials taskss! Wess bes thes oness tos findss thes peopless! Wess bes thes oness tos makess Alethiess fallss!"

There was a rousing cheer which sounded a bit like the low notes on a piano thumped hard and inharmoniously together.

Harris stared at the creatures in horror. Aletheia! They wanted Aletheia to fall! Incredibly, he had stumbled across a meeting of the enemies of the city his brother, Jack, had taught him to love. What had happened to Jack? Had he come here too and been taken captive by these awful savages? The most enormous monsters could have gobbled him up! He looked around the flickering chamber. There were plenty of tunnels, similar to the one through which he had crawled, leading to and from the cavern. Many of them were far bigger too, which he assumed was how some of the larger brutes arrived in this place.

"Wheres hass thes Alethiess peopless goness, ohs Greatss Oness?" asked a tall creature respectfully.

"Wess ssearchess undergroundss!" thundered the leader.

At this point there was another rousing cheer, and a particularly loud hissing ogre offered what Harris interpreted to be three cheers for 'the Masters'.

"Wess wills takess sshapess ands findss thes Alethiess ssecretss!" The leader pointed at a creature who sat close by, appearing perhaps more human-like than the others present. He was even dressed in what could, on a person, have been badly fitted trousers and a shirt.

This one sat in silence through the whole meeting, as if disdainful of the behaviour of the others. "Oldiemanss willss bes thes firsts tos changess! Hess willss advancess ands opens thes ways!"

The mutant named 'Oldieman' looked unsurprised at the announcement. As Harris watched in horrified fascination, Oldieman's form began to change. His bulbous eyes and shapeless body smoothed and slithered and shrank and twisted and turned, with grunts and groans accompanying the whole, terrifying performance. And then, standing in the midst of the terrible company, there was something that, in the poor, flickering light, resembled an old man.

"Tos Alethiess!" cried the leader.

"Downss withs Alethiesss!" echoed the monsters.

The wretch Oldieman – apparently so named for the old man he could resemble – walked with strange, jerky, unnatural movements towards a tunnel at the side of the cavern. And then he was gone.

Harris sat in terror through the whole performance, crouching behind his rock. He had never been so scared in his life. Jack had described his adventures in Aletheia with the Snares and other frightening creatures, but Harris never realised how it felt to be facing the enemies of Aletheia, the enemies of the Truth of the Bible. Harris had trusted in the Lord Jesus and was very glad to be a Christian[1]. He badly wanted to do his bit and fight as a Christian, but he never anticipated facing these horrible enemies on his own. He had no idea what could have happened to Aletheia and why they talked about it being underground; he only knew that somehow he must stop all these brutes from leaving this place to cause harm to the city he had never seen, but learned to love.

He remembered Jack talking about the power of prayer, and, as more of the enemies of Aletheia started to take human-like shapes, he began to pray. More than anything he prayed to be able to stop these savages from finding Aletheia. And then, heedless of drawing attention to himself, he rummaged frantically in his rucksack for his Bible – which was one of the essential supplies he had been carrying around in preparation for the longed-for adventure in Aletheia.

His fumbling, trembling hand closed around his Bible just as the nearest creature noticed him. It was in the middle of a transformation from one thing to another and one eye was quite tiny, while the other was far too large. Its mismatched eyes stared at Harris in what could only have been an expression of stupid bewilderment. Amidst the grunts and groans of the creatures shifting shape into a weird army of trouble-makers, the wretch cried, "Boyss! Humanss!"

"Sspiess!" cried a humungous fiend lumbering clumsily towards Harris.

"Wess ares betrayedss!" cried another.

More quickly than you could imagine shapeless, changing, writhing mutants moving, they were heading towards Harris, and, before he could even think to scuttle up the small pipe, he was completely surrounded.

He had but one weapon: only the Bible, the Word of God, stood between him and this motley throng.

"Sspeakss!" thundered the leader, pushing through the other beings to stare down at the small boy before him. The leader's shape had nearly finished changing. He was a large, fierce-looking man, still completing the transformation by sprouting a thick, black beard. Harris didn't have any idea how this man-like beast expected to go unnoticed amongst the folk of Aletheia. Perhaps they were intended to be an army of fighters. "Howss dids yous comes heress?" cried the leader, clenching his fist.

"I won't tell you!" said Harris, with far more boldness than he felt.

"Youss daress tos defiess messs…!" The large, hairy, bulging and not-quite-human hand reached towards him.

Harris pulled his Bible from the confines of his rucksack and into the open. Radiant light suddenly spilled in bright beams from its pages, into the darkest corners of the cavern. Harris hadn't seen real, literal light shine from his Bible[6]; he had only heard Jack describe this from his adventures in Aletheia. And now, in delight, he watched the warm, golden light send his enemies backwards in utter confusion and dismay. Instead of thunderous low notes of cheering celebration, the creatures emitted high-pitched screeches, trying desperately to escape the all-seeing light that cast no shadows for hiding. They rushed for the exits furthest away from Harris, some shuffling, some limping, some crawling, some slithering, as their limbs still shifted and changed.

BOOM!

With a terrifying roar, rocks began to block the exits from the cavern. Massive boulders crumbled and fell and rolled down from the roof, all around the edge of the cave. Harris, his Bible still in his hand, crouched in the entrance of the small pipe through which he had crawled to this strange meeting, helpless to do anything but pray. But no stones fell on him. No rocks tumbled to block his exit.

When the noise ceased, and the dust and debris settled, the bright light of the Bible showed a horrible sight. Dozens of monsters lay broken and dead beneath the rubble in the cavern. Others groaned and limped and staggered towards the small boy who blocked what was now the only way out. The creatures which remained were no longer changing into human-like shapes. Whatever power allowed them to do that was disrupted in the rock-fall. Instead, the large bulbous shapes shrivelled and shrank until they were all long, and thin, and slithering, like large, horrible snakes.

Harris scooped up his rucksack, and, holding the Bible in his hand, began to move backwards, up the narrow pipe, to the entrance from the ditch. He wondered if anyone in his quiet, uneventful village of Steeple-Bumpton had any idea what was happening beneath the ground!

He reached the top of the pipe and scuttled across the area of earth and stones and old leaves until his back hit the small, wooden, number seventeen door. Down the pipe, beyond the rays of light which still shone from the Bible, he could hear the slithering noises of dozens of the mutants which still remained, making their way through the pipe towards him. In their current form, as large, elongated snake-like beings, they would have no problem navigating the pipe.

Harris saw the first bulbous eyes peering at him beyond the brightest beams of light.

"Letss uss throughss!" hissed the snake. "Wess meanss nos harmss tos yousss!"

Harris held his Bible close to the mouth of the pipe and the serpent hissed angrily. "You mean harm to Aletheia," he said boldly. "And I will never let you through!"

He wasn't sure how these creatures could get to Aletheia since the cavern was well and truly blocked; but he would never let them escape and find another way to harm the city. He leaned back against the wooden door and watched the entrance to the pipe. He was thankful there was still some food in his rucksack from his school lunch earlier. It was all the healthy stuff that was left – an apple, some grapes and a banana, but it was still better than nothing. He was damp and cold. He had no idea where Jack was or how and when he would return.

But, with his Bible in his hand, Harris would guard and contain the enemies of Aletheia.

For as long as he was able.

CHAPTER 20
BENJAMIN ESCAPES

Jack and Zek put on their armour of God[11] and prepared for their first guard duty at Justification. They wanted everything to be exactly right. They were very grateful to Bourne for allowing them to continue on guard duty – albeit supervised and not on the farmlands – and were determined to be found worthy. This time they would not do anything that might be breaking the rules. Hector was tied under an archway at Foundation-of-Faith Apartments, puzzled and upset at being left behind. He would annoy all the neighbours for the duration of Zek's absence, whining and barking to be set free.

The boys left nice and early and walked to the underground entry point of Justification. This was guarded even underground, and the boys would need a Rescuer to decode the door that barred the way to this precious Bible Truth. They found Benjamin Wright loitering at the corner of the street.

"Hello, Ben!" said Zek. He liked his older cousin; Benjamin was always cheerful and good fun. But today Benjamin looked glum.

"Where are you going?" he asked.

"It's our first guard duty at Justification," said Zek.

"Did you ask if I could help too?" asked Benjamin.

"Uh, oh, sorry, Ben," said Zek. "We haven't had a chance to talk to Bourne about that, he's so busy, and…"

"Perhaps I could tag along with you?" suggested Benjamin hopefully.

Zek and Jack looked uncertainly at each other. They were going to be so careful to do everything just right, and both of them instinctively knew this did *not* include letting Ben go with them without proper permission.

"Perhaps if you asked Mr Mustardpot?" suggested Jack. The big Headmaster was technically still in charge of the children, and, although he was often scary, he was also a very fair-minded man.

"He wouldn't let me," said Benjamin gloomily. "He's making me work non-stop at the Food Distribution Centre, keeping me out of trouble, he says!"

Zek grinned. Benjamin was known for getting into scrapes of one kind or another.

"It's not funny, Zek," said Ben. "I'm bored stiff with apples and pears and plums and potatoes! It's all old folk working there, and most of them are nuts! I've got two hours off – just two hours! I must do something interesting for once!"

"You could ask Henry if she could talk to Bourne for you," suggested Jack. "You know she's working for Bourne now…"

Benjamin shrugged helplessly. "It's worth a try, I suppose," he said. "And if not, then I'll have to sort things out myself!"

Jack and Zek watched the retreating figure. "Will he do something crazy?" asked Jack.

Zek nodded. "He might," he said.

Benjamin made a half-hearted effort to locate his cousin Henrietta to ask her to intercede for him with Bourne. When ten minutes of his precious two hours of free time had passed, he decided he dare not wait any longer; he would carry out his own plan. He had often done so in the past, usually at the instigation of his friend, Charlie Steady. Although there were usually consequences, none had been so serious that they lingered in his mind as a deterrent. Mr Mustardpot was, of course, a formidable opponent, but if all went to plan, no one but the kids would know what he had done; and they wouldn't tell tales. Besides, his idea, to scare them from the *outside* of Justification, was something they would probably thoroughly enjoy.

Benjamin knew there were ways to get into aboveground Aletheia without adult permission. He would merely shadow a Rescuer going on duty for aboveground missions. It was surprising to him that there weren't, after all, many locks and bolts and codes and passwords between him and the outside world, except in odd places like

Justification. The Rescuers were so busy on their rescuing missions to The Outskirts that the discreet exits from the Academy of Soldiers-of-the-Cross onto the streets of Aletheia were constantly in use. The prayer power was still steadily increasing, and as it increased, so did the missions to rescue people. The invaders of the land of Err were oblivious to the folk who slipped down alleyways, and through archways, and into small doorways of which there were dozens around the massive fortress. In fact, the light of the Bible the Rescuers held blinded the people of Err to any sight of an entrance into the fortress they could not overcome.

The young Rescuer whom Benjamin chose to follow was particularly, if inadvertently, helpful. He was late for his duty and hurried through the passageways of the Academy, glancing with evident concern at his watch as he went. At last he reached a small door set into the thick stone wall. Benjamin slipped behind a shiny suit of armour which stood conveniently close by. He watched as the Rescuer removed his Bible and pressed it into the indentation in the door. A small, clear *click*. And silently the door opened. The Rescuer slipped through the doorway and Benjamin heard the call of another Rescuer beyond the door, teasing his friend for being late. And then, quick as a flash, Benjamin leapt from behind the suit of armour and caught the door just before it clicked shut again.

He stood still and silent for a moment, listening to the noise of the Rescuers retreating into the distance. Then he poked his head cautiously around the door and took his first deep breath of aboveground air in months. It was raining in Aletheia and he relished the cold, fresh dampness. He slipped outside and placed the small sliver of wood from his pocket into the opening of the door. Then he looked around.

When Benjamin entered aboveground Aletheia he found himself in a secluded passageway with high, stone walls on either side of him, stretching up into one of the many towers of the fortress Academy which soared above. There was no one in sight. Cautiously, but with increasing confidence, he walked down the passageway to the opening at the end and stared at the scene before him.

There was a fair on what was once Pride Way. People jostled and chattered and called to each other, sheltering from the rain under the coverings of stalls. There were trinkets, and household items, and clothes, and food stalls. There was a stand called 'The Greasy Cook' which sold hotdogs and sausage rolls. Despite the dubious appearance of the man behind the counter, Benjamin secretly wished he had money to buy some food. It was definitely more interesting than the rationed fruit and vegetables of underground Aletheia!

There were important-looking people wearing suits and holding umbrellas, scrutinising the Judges' Academy and scribbling notes. There were groups of teenagers and kids. There were workmen and women, taking a break from whatever they were involved with elsewhere in Aletheia and enjoying the fair. There was even a tired-looking merry-go-round which offered rides and from which emanated out-of-tune music.

Benjamin took a deep breath and walked cautiously into the fair, trying to blend in. To his surprise, no one took any notice of him at all. He became braver and wandered amongst the stalls, shrugging or grinning at anyone who tried to sell him something, pleased when they obviously accepted him as one of themselves.

When he moved away from the market stalls and further up the road to Redemption Square, no one noticed. He simply blended in with the people who walked in that direction. He wished he had thought to wear a jacket on his venture into the cold, damp autumn afternoon, but otherwise he was undismayed by the changed world of aboveground Aletheia. It was dreadful, of course, what the invaders were doing to his home city. And he was still determined to do his best to drive the invaders out. But it was also exciting to realise he could, after all, explore quite safely amongst them.

Until he stood on the edge of Redemption Square.

Benjamin came to an abrupt halt. In the past, he never thought of Redemption Square the way the others did. It was a nice, peaceful place, but it didn't mean much else to him. Benjamin knew the people of Aletheia thought of it as the most important place in their lives. He had never thought of it as *that*. But he was filled with a feeling of sadness at the sight of it now. The peace and tranquillity were shattered. The space was a muddled encampment of people who filled the square with tents and rough shelters. They had lit bonfires too, and Benjamin saw there were banners and slogans around the square. One, close by where he stood, read, 'Let Err into Aletheia!' It was a rather odd banner, thought Benjamin, since it was obvious that Err was already in Aletheia! Across the square was the place he hoped to reach – to play a harmless prank on Zek and Jack, and Hugo and Timmy too. The building of Justification, with its majestic stone pillars, was untouched by the people in the square. They could not enter and shelter there. Instead, they blocked the way. And Benjamin could go no further.

CHAPTER 21
MR CON COZEN

Rather gloomily, Benjamin retraced his steps through the fair and stood once more at the end of the small passageway through which he entered the city. But he was startled to discover that this way, also, was blocked. Not by a protest camp, but only by a very old man who slumped by the entrance, almost as if he was asleep. Benjamin stepped cautiously over the man, wondering whether he needed help. He was by nature very kind, and it was a shame such a frail old man should be enduring the chill of the autumn rain.

Just then, the old man stirred. He got slowly to his feet, moving in strange, jerky motions, as if he was extremely stiff. "E-excuses me, boys," he said, in a quavering voice with a peculiar accent.

"Are you alright?" asked Benjamin kindly. He wondered how he could get away from the man and go down the passageway to the door which he had wedged open.

"A-a-alrightss?" stammered the old man. Iss v-verys w-wets throughs!"

"Uh, right, I can see that," said Benjamin. "Are you-are you a friend of Aletheia?" he ventured. He was feeling decidedly out of his depth, trying to figure out what to do with this old man.

"F-friends? A-Aletheiass?" The old man laughed, as if Benjamin had told a good joke. "S-soons there iss no f-friends!" he said.

Benjamin frowned. Usually people were more optimistic than that. "Well, I know it's in a pretty bad state," he said. "But it's not finished yet!"

"I l-l-lookings for t-the undergrounds places, p-pleases," the old man said, changing the subject and suddenly looking anxiously around and about him.

Benjamin regarded him with interest. "Have they rescued you and left you here?" he asked.

"R-r-rescued…y-yess, that'ss its," stuttered the old man.

"What's your name?" asked Benjamin.

"Cons Cozens," said the old man more firmly.

Benjamin was intrigued. As far as oddness went, this old man was a match for even Dim View, and his name sounded like he hailed from abroad – which might explain his peculiar accent. "I'm Benjamin Wright," said Benjamin. "Where do you come from?"

"C-comes froms?" stuttered Mr Cozen in his strange voice.

"Perhaps from No-Witness Apartments on The Outskirts?" ventured Benjamin, wondering if a theme of weirdness ran through all the people that once lived there.

"Y-yess," said Mr Cozen vaguely. "But I needs to g-gets…"

"Underground," agreed Benjamin. "Yeah, I know." It was rather satisfying to be in the position of helping with a rescue. He felt he was doing something important at last, like the others doing their guard duty. "I expect they'll put you in with the other oldies, Mr Cozen," he commented as the old man took his arm. "I mean," he corrected himself, "with the, uh, other slightly older people who work in the Food Distribution Centre."

He was surprised how strong Con Cozen's grip was on his arm as they moved down the passageway. Perhaps there was more to the unknown Mr Cozen than the shapeless clothing and uncomfortable walking showed. "I work there too," Benjamin confided. "I'll take you with me now; I'm due back there…" He glanced at his watch. "Well, I'm due back *now!*" he exclaimed. The two free hours were gone. Benjamin hoped Mr Mustardpot was not at the Centre today.

Mr Cozen seemed happy to leave his fate in Benjamin's hands. They entered through the side door into the Academy without encountering any difficulty, and Benjamin slipped the handy sliver of wood back into his pocket. Once they were inside the Academy, Mr Cozen seemed to recover. He was still frail and old, but he released his clutch on Benjamin and was able to walk on his own. They saw no one on their journey through the Academy to the Food Distribution Centre. Everyone was busy with their duties.

"I expect you'll be put on the food assembly line," said Benjamin. He didn't over-think the matter. He knew there was paperwork and stuff like that somewhere, and Mr Straw and his assistants were often checking lists and writing rotas and counting things. But paperwork wasn't one of Benjamin's strong points: he just assumed the folk who managed the Food Distribution Centre would be happy with an extra pair of hands. It might even mean they would release him for more interesting jobs, like guard duty!

He slipped to his place – still counting apples – just as his shift was about to start. '*Mrs De Voté: 2 apples*' was the first item on the list, and he deftly placed two in the correct section of the box and pushed it down the line to Mr Dim View who was, as usual, earnestly studying his list.

"You see," said Benjamin cheerfully to Mr Cozen, who was hovering close to his elbow and darting anxious glances left, right and centre. "You see, there's not much to it. Now, watch Mr View here, and he will put the number of pears that Mrs De Voté wants into the box."

Mr View scrutinised his list anxiously, and Benjamin sighed and peered over Dim View's shoulder. "Mrs De Voté doesn't want any pears, Mr View," he said patiently. "That happens sometimes," he explained to Mr Cozen. "You'll get the hang of it. Now, do you want to do the next one on the list? That's…Mr Upright. See? He wants three apples…"

Mr Cozen fumbled with the apples and knocked two on the floor, which rolled and bounced their way to the 'potatoes' section of the assembly line, confusing the old lady there who could barely tell the difference. Benjamin imagined apples tucked in among the potatoes and sighed with frustration. Con Cozen cautiously picked up an apple and placed it in the box. He looked questioningly at Benjamin.

"Two more," said Benjamin. He began to wonder if the old man could count. Rather optimistically, he still hoped Mr Cozen would, at some unspecified point in the future, be able to replace him on the food assembly line. He just needed a little training.

But something unexpected happened quite suddenly.

Dim View reached for his battered Bible which was always close by his hand. Benjamin could not tell what made Mr View reach for his Bible at that moment. The odd, old man seemed to have taken an instant dislike to the equally odd, old Mr Cozen. Light spilled from the Bible, across the pears, onto the apples that Mr Cozen was lifting carefully into the box.

With startling swiftness, Mr Cozen upset the apple box entirely, and fled helter-skelter for the nearest exit.

"Well, I never," said Benjamin, staring after him. He wondered whether he was bound to go after the old man and rescue him once more, but Mr Mustardpot put an inadvertent stop to that by suddenly appearing at the food assembly line. Benjamin was loath to give the Headmaster cause to doubt him; he was still hoping to be given a better job.

"Well, Wright," said Mr Mustardpot, stopping by 'apples'. "Has there been an accident here?"

"Uh, only a small one, sir," said Benjamin.

Mr Mustardpot gamely helped to pick up the scattered apples, examining one or two and frowning over their bruises. "I hope you spent your free time profitably this afternoon, Wright," said the Headmaster. Benjamin sighed. He had actually rescued someone that very afternoon, and still they must doubt him! He conveniently forgot he had originally gone aboveground to play a trick on his friends. They set the box on the table. "And how are you getting on, Mr View?" asked Mr Mustardpot, turning to the old man next to Benjamin.

Mr View wasn't getting on very well at all. He was tightly clutching his Bible and staring fixedly at the exit through which the strange Mr Cozen had vanished.

Benjamin busied himself with the apples, quickly placing the required number in the box. He hoped he looked diligent – and innocent too. What had got into funny Mr View? Surely he wouldn't give Benjamin away. For, as pleased as Benjamin was to have rescued someone, he couldn't admit to it without also admitting he had gone aboveground without permission.

"Are you quite well, Mr View?" asked Mr Mustardpot kindly. For all his big, blustery ways, Mr Mustardpot was always very kind to the older people.

Mr View pointed to the exit with his big, old, battered Bible. Strong light shone the way he pointed. "He went that way," said Mr View.

"I see," said Mr Mustardpot. He hesitated, as if he wondered whether to ask more. But Mr View was often muddled over things. The Headmaster moved on down the assembly line, commenting, praising, encouraging, making them smile. He didn't hear the last word Mr View uttered. Benjamin was the only one who heard it, and he didn't understand.

"Spy!" said Dim View.

CHAPTER 22
BETRAYED!

Rain lashed against the high windows of the meeting room. Mr Philologus Mustardpot drummed his fingers on the old timbers of the table before him. This Management Meeting was meant to be good news. The defence of Aletheia, the attack to take back the city, was ready to be unleashed. Everything was in place.

But, instead, the news was grim.

Mr Mustardpot took some satisfaction from picturing the invaders and workforce and holidaymakers of Err getting drenched in yet another autumn storm. A roll of thunder rumbled ominously in the distance and he nodded with fierce approval at the imaginary picture of the campsites on the Pray-Always Farmlands being washed away, sent tumbling and spluttering down the soaking fields, all the way back over the boundaries of Aletheia in a frantic, rushing deluge.

Sturdy Wright, the Head Keeper of the Water of Sound Doctrine, was looking stunned. He was distraught. In utter disbelief. After all, if the defences of the underground had been breached, and food was missing, was their precious supply of Water of Sound Doctrine also compromised? "Are we absolutely certain our underground defences have been breached?" he asked huskily.

The Chief of Aletheia nodded grimly from his place at the head of the table. "I'm afraid that's the only conclusion we can come to," he said. "We have explored every other explanation for the missing food supplies, and there is no other way to account for it. Our prayer power is good and growing every day. We've almost reached the level we would wish to take back the city."

"Mr Straw and Mr Mustardpot have carefully examined their records of food rations and supplies," continued Captain Steadfast from the Chief's right hand. "They have been meticulous in their calculations and the figures don't add up. Valuable supplies are missing."

Mr Mustardpot nodded grimly. Mr Straw, who was seated by his side, had a ferocious frown on his face. He had broken the delicate handle off his coffee cup and was fiddling with it absentmindedly.

"And I'm afraid there's something else which leads us to the conclusion that we have a problem."

There was a hush in the vast room. All the managers held their collective breath, and Mr Sturdy Wright put his head in his hands as if he could not bear to hear more. "We now have conclusive proof that some of our Pray-Always Farmlands supplies have not only been, uh, stolen, but some have even been *contaminated*."

"Contaminated!" There was an explosion of sound across the room

– ripples of shock and protest that there could possibly be someone, *anyone*, in their midst who would sabotage the supplies of the city.

"How, Chief?" asked Hardy Wallop, as shocked as everyone else.

"A quantity of our seed for spring crops – thankfully only a small quantity so far – is dying," said the Chief soberly. "And blight has been injected into some of the fruit. I'll let Dr Pentone, who has analysed it, explain a bit more about the technicalities."

There was strained silence in the room as Dr Theo Pentone, in a rumpled, dubiously-stained lab coat, got to his feet. He was the Director of Health and also the Chief Scientist of Aletheia, and was widely accepted to be the cleverest man in the city – although he looked like nothing of the sort. He oversaw a team of doctors and scientists who worked in his department in the Academy, but he dealt with this grave matter personally. "I have reason to believe that the blight introduced into the fruit is the same, or very similar, to the blight the Fretters attempted to use to attack the Pray-Always Farmlands back in the spring," he said bluntly. "You'll all remember the, uh, heroic efforts of two boys to prevent that attack, in the course of which they were both bitten and poisoned with Fretter-blight-poison."[3]

People nodded grimly. The spring felt like a long time ago now the city was so beleaguered. But they all remembered that Jack

Merryweather and Hezekiah Wallop had managed to capture a Fretter leader, which had prevented the most terrible catastrophe on the farmlands.

"I was able, through that incident, to extract and retain two samples of the Fretter poison," said Dr Pentone. "One from the boys, and one from the Fretter leader. I have analysed these samples, and it is absolutely consistent with the blight recently introduced into our food supplies."

"Has anyone been affected by the blight?" someone asked faintly.

Dr Pentone nodded soberly. "We've seen green-tinge – which is one of the symptoms – on a couple of people already," he said.

The Chief rose slowly to his feet. "We have no option but to consider that…" he paused, as if he could hardly bring himself to say the next words. "…that we have an enemy in our midst," he concluded huskily.

The unthinkable had happened.

Aletheia had been betrayed!

CHAPTER 23
INVESTIGATION

Of course, the Management Meeting did not end there. Irrefutable evidence had been provided by Mr Straw, Mr Mustardpot and Dr Pentone that there was a sabotage-spy in underground Aletheia. Now there must be an investigation and a plan to catch the spy. Time was pressing. They must stop the saboteur; and they must be ready for the fight for aboveground Aletheia before the Council of Err and the creatures of Err discovered their underground refuge. Even now, information might be winging its way to the Council of Err from the unknown spy.

Hardy Wallop, pale and chewing anxiously on his moustache, felt ill with dismay at this intrusion into underground Aletheia. The security of entry into Aletheia was his department.

"Don't take this personally, Hardy," said the Chief. "None of us think any less of you. Perhaps we have all let our guard down, thinking we were ready to take back our city. We knew our enemies would attempt to sabotage us."

"But I thought I had everything covered," muttered Mr Wallop. "I was so certain…"

"Uh, I hate to ask this, Hardy," said the Chief Judge, Sagacia

Steady, peering over her sparkly spectacles down the table at him. "But I suppose the breach in security couldn't have happened when the boy, Jack Merryweather, arrived in underground Aletheia?"

Hardy Wallop shook his head. "I'd stake my life on it," he said. "And it's interesting to me that Jack's brother, who was intending to follow him, hasn't yet appeared in Aletheia."

"You mean, you think the other Merryweather boy was somehow stopped?"

Hardy Wallop nodded slowly. "Once Jack told me his brother might be coming, I've had folk watching for him," he said. "I can only conclude that the entry through which Jack came was subsequently blocked."

"Perhaps his brother is guarding the way," suggested a senior Rescuer hopefully. Had they known how small Harris Merryweather was, they might not have thought such a thing could be possible.

"What other 'breaches' in security have we had recently, Chief?" asked Mr Wallop anxiously.

"I've summoned Lieutenant Bourne Faithful to the meeting with an update on this," answered the Chief. He looked at the clock, and, right on cue, Lieutenant Faithful knocked on the door.

Bourne Faithful entered and saluted the company. Accompanying Bourne, looking slightly bemused, was a boy with messy hair, thick-rimmed glasses, and an earnest, pleasing expression. "Go ahead, Lieutenant," said the Chief, glancing with slight speculation at the boy who was dressed in a lab coat of the Central Control Room.

"We have a report from the Central Mission Detector of all the breaches in security, concerning underground, Bible-access-only doors and entry points, which have taken place over the past few weeks," said Bourne. "With me is Dusty Addle." He gestured to the boy who accompanied him, who raised a hand and waved sheepishly, then clearly wished he hadn't. "Dusty has been working in the Control Room, and knows about an incident which is relevant to this investigation – which we'll come to presently."

Bourne shuffled his papers and found the one he wanted. "In summary, there were a total of twelve breaches in security over the period in question. Of these, eight are matters of maintenance or other explainable faults and failings which were quickly resolved. I have no reason to think there is any possibility that any of these have caused the, uh, *problem* we now face."

Understandably, he stumbled over the word 'problem'. It was such a gigantic, such an unthinkable event, they were all still reeling from the shock of it.

"Which leaves four incidents which might give us a clue as to how this *spy* got underground and who he is," growled Mr Mustardpot, who was hanging on every word.

Bourne truly did not want to mention the incident involving Jack and Zek at Mr Croft Straw's farmhouse, but he knew he must. He briefly outlined the excursion of two 'young Rescuers' (he didn't name them, but Jack and Zek would have been delighted to be referred to as real Rescuers), who went aboveground onto the farmlands in response to what they felt was an emergency.

The Chief frowned, and Mr Straw raised his eyebrows. Bourne had a hunch the farmer knew to whom he was referring. "But you're satisfied, Lieutenant, that this particular incident could not have led to the person these two Rescuers met in, uh, a barn, entering underground Aletheia?"

"Reasonably satisfied, sir," said Bourne. "Dusty Addle, here, faithfully reported the incident, and I sent Rescuers on additional patrols in that part of underground Aletheia for the next few days."

The Chief nodded. "The other incidents?"

The next two of the four incidents were also adequately explained. Which left only one.

"I brought Dusty Addle with me because it is due to his diligence and quick thinking that we are alerted to this seemingly innocuous incident – which might have otherwise gone unnoticed."

Everyone in the room paid attention. Candour Communique was sitting on the edge of her seat. She had the most dreadful sinking feeling that her request to allow two untrained Rescuers, Hugo Wallop and Timmy Trial, to visit The Outskirts had somehow led to this terrible betrayal. Josie Faithful's notes on their subsequent adventure and the rescue of Dim View made interesting reading. But it was clear to Candour the boys were on their own for sufficient time to perhaps inadvertently do something to jeopardise the underground city. When it was obvious the incident was nothing to do with this, Candour sank back in her seat in utter relief. She did not dare to look at Captain Steadfast. Had he remembered the request too and thought her actions might have endangered Aletheia?

Bourne Faithful finished speaking and Candour once more paid attention.

"You mean that an outside, Bible-access-only door into the

Academy of Soldiers-of-the-Cross was open for over an hour?!" exclaimed the Chief.

"Not wide open, sir," said Bourne.

"What difference does that make?" retorted the Chief. "It still means that someone – anyone! – could have entered the Academy in that time and gone…anywhere!"

"Agreed," said Bourne grimly. "But the difference, sir, and this is why Dusty's remarkable diligence is noteworthy, is that on our systems in the Control Room, this breach of security barely registered as a breach at all. The door was *almost* shut, and the faintly flickering light on the panel in the Control Room could have been overlooked."

"Well done, young man!" boomed Mr Mustardpot.

Dusty smiled self-consciously.

"We think it was wedged open," said Bourne bluntly. "That door – Door Nineteen – was recently maintained. There was no reason it wouldn't close properly."

There was further shock in the room. Someone from underground Aletheia had truly been that careless? Was it remotely possible there was an enemy within? Not everyone who lived in underground Aletheia was a Christian. Some were there because they were children, and their families lived there; a few had lived amongst Aletheians all their lives. But it seemed inconceivable that any of them would want to risk underground Aletheia!

"Can we have the date and exact timings of this particular breach, Lieutenant?" asked the Chief briskly. "I think, in the absence of anything else, we must follow this up thoroughly. And we need the identities and shifts of the Rescuers using Door Nineteen around that time. I suppose we can tell who last exited the door before it didn't close properly? That might possibly be the very person who wedged it open!"

"I've already prepared this information, sir," said Bourne, stepping forward and handing him a report.

The Chief flicked through the report. The rest of the room watched in silence as his eyes lighted on the named Rescuer who last exited through the door.

"I suppose," said the Chief slowly, "that the young Private named on this report has already been interviewed by you, Lieutenant?"

"Yes, sir," said Bourne, and the Chief almost smiled. Bourne Faithful was a rising star in the Rescuers. Once, long ago now, no one would ever have thought Bourne Faithful would stand for the Truth. But he was a living example of what the grace of God could do, and the scar on his face was testimony of it. Now he was one of the most reliable Lieutenants in the force.

"And?" prompted the Chief, pushing the report across to Captain Steadfast. The Captain quickly scanned it and shut the report firmly.

"I have absolute confidence in the Rescuer concerned," said Bourne.

"As have I," said the Captain firmly.

"If we rule out the Rescuer named in this report, what other person could have done this?" asked the Chief.

"Someone who followed and waited for the opportunity," said Bourne. "The Rescuer said he was in a hurry and didn't look back to see if the door was shut. Many of us have done that, sir."

"Quite," said the Chief. "And there is no other Rescuer registered in the Control Room as exiting through that door?"

"None."

"Then we're searching for a non-Rescuer who won't be on our systems," said the Chief.

"Chief," said Mr Mustardpot slowly, "would it be possible for me to see the report on the date and time of the breach?"

The Chief passed the report to the Headmaster. "You have an idea, Philologus?" he asked.

Mr Mustardpot noted the information in silence. He had an excellent memory for times and dates. He knew exactly what had happened at the time mentioned on the report. "Perhaps I do, Chief," he said.

CHAPTER 24
SUSPECTS

The children congregated in the underground portion of their school and sat on the classroom chairs which were clustered there. Occasionally this area had been used for teaching the children that remained in the city. But that was before all hands were needed to fight for Aletheia, and no lessons had been held here for some time. But, on the very few occasions they all had time off together, it was a convenient place to meet. And there was only one subject amongst them to discuss. The news was out. There was a spy in underground Aletheia!

"I took the report of the security breaches to Bourne myself," said Henrietta.

"Did you read it?" asked Timmy.

"No, of course not," said Henrietta. "Bourne's very strict about such things!"

"That's a pity," said Timmy frankly. "I wonder what was in it."

"Well, Dusty can tell us *that*," said Henrietta.

Dusty, who was no good at hiding anything, went a dull, awkward red. "I can't," he said desperately. "You know I would tell you if I could, but Bourne was very straight about this report. They don't want anyone knowing the details of the breaches or anything, so they can catch the person, you see?"

"I don't see how it will help to catch the spy," said Henrietta.

"But don't worry about not being able to tell us, Dusty," said Hugo kindly. Dusty, who admired Henrietta very much, was looking crestfallen that he couldn't share the details with them all.

"How did the managers in the meeting react to the report?" Henrietta asked eagerly.

Dusty had not been told not to say anything about *that*. He was glad he could answer. "They were shocked," he said. Even an unobservant person could not have missed the tense dismay of the managers in the meeting.

"Was Mr Straw there?" asked Zek anxiously.

"Yes," said Dusty. He knew what Zek and Jack, both very pale, were thinking. They were remembering the breach in security they caused at Mr Straw's house; they were wondering whether it was them who were responsible for the entry of the spy. Dusty wished he could reassure them; but he could not.

"We think it might all be our fault," said Jack bravely.

"You?" exclaimed Henrietta. "You mean when you came into Aletheia, Jack?"

"No, not that," said Jack, now beginning to wonder if his entry into underground Aletheia had, indeed, caused the security breach.

"It was when Jack and I went on guard duty at Mr Straw's farmhouse," said Zek.

The others had, by now, heard the full account of this.

"I don't think it'll be your fault," said Hugo. "I think they would have come to question you if they thought you could, uh, help with this."

"You don't actually *know* that, Hugo," said Henrietta. Hugo glared at her, and when she caught the uncertain expression on the two younger boys' faces, she subsided into silence.

"Anyway," said Timmy, "it might equally be Hugo and I who are to blame!"

Hugo nodded grimly. "We've been thinking about that girl, Crystal, and how she might have followed us to an underground entry point after all," he said. "Perhaps that was in the report." He glanced at Dusty, who was looking steadily at his shoes.

"Well, if it comes to that, *I'm* to blame for that one too!" said Josie. "It was my idea to get you two to go aboveground!"

"It looks like most of us are to blame!" said Henrietta. "I'm probably to blame too, through the apple throwing incident!"

"I don't think so, Henry," said Hugo.

"Dusty *isn't* to blame, that's for sure," said Henrietta. Dusty beamed.

"And Ben? What about you? I don't suppose you've been up to much, since you're stuck in the Food Distribution Centre!"

"Thanks for reminding me!" said Benjamin, but he was grinning at his cousin. "But I *do* have an idea about who it *might* be," he added.

Henrietta giggled. Then stopped. "Are you serious?" she asked.

Benjamin nodded. "I've been watching him over the last few days," he said. "He's behaving oddly – not that that's anything remarkable – but I just have a feeling…"

"Who?" asked Josie eagerly. She wondered about a story! Could *The Truth* newspaper be the first to break the story about the spy in underground Aletheia?

"I don't think I should say…yet," said Benjamin mysteriously.

"Have you told someone else about it?" asked Henrietta. "If you can't tell us, you *must* tell Mr Straw or Mr Mustardpot at the Food Distribution Centre before all the food is ruined!"

"I don't think one spy could ruin *all* the food that quickly, Henry," said Hugo.

"You don't know there's only *one* spy," said Henrietta darkly. "There could be a whole spy ring!"

"I don't think so, Henry," said Hugo.

"But you must tell someone, Ben," said Josie seriously. "You really must!"

CHAPTER 25
INTERVIEW WITH MR MUSTARDPOT

Benjamin pondered the tricky problem of telling someone in authority about his suspicions regarding the spy. Because the spy was focussing on sabotaging the food supplies, attention was turning towards the Food Distribution Centre, and, at last, Benjamin felt his job was becoming interesting. There might soon be plenty of action around him, and he felt sure he could play a key role in catching the spy. He watched his suspect closely. The old man's behaviour was even more peculiar than it was before. He was anxious, paranoid, always on the look-out, and, if more proof were needed, he also talked about spies!

When Mr Mustardpot approached Benjamin at the end of his shift at the Centre the following day, he watched as the boy diligently tidied the 'apples' corner. "I'd like a word, please, Wright," he said.

In the past, in his scrapes at school, 'a word' with Mr Mustardpot was never a good thing. But, since Mr Mustardpot was unlikely to have anything to be concerned about in his recent exemplary behaviour, even putting in extra hours at the Food Distribution Centre to gather evidence against his suspect, Benjamin agreed politely. He followed

Mr Mustardpot to Mr Straw's makeshift office which was in a corner of the massive food storage space.

Mr Mustardpot took a seat behind the desk. "Sit down, Wright," he said.

Benjamin took a seat in front of the messy table. It was like being back in the Headmaster's office. And yet it was not quite the same. "I've got something I want to tell you, sir," said Benjamin promptly.

Mr Mustardpot, who was seldom taken off guard, was astonished. "Do you?" he asked. He wondered if he had worried unnecessarily about getting the truth from Benjamin Wright about this most important breach in security. He didn't want to involve his already extremely anxious father, Sturdy Wright. He only wanted the truth of exactly where Benjamin was during the all-important hour when the entry door was wedged open.

It wasn't that Benjamin wasn't honest: he was. But he could talk around subjects until he was blue in the face, and never answer questions at all. But it was surely too much of a coincidence that Benjamin Wright, prankster and mischief-maker, had two free hours at exactly that time! It would be typical of Benjamin's past escapades to do something like this, to go aboveground on a whim or for a prank. Usually his pranks involved his close friend, Charlie Steady. Thankfully, in Mr Mustardpot's opinion, Charlie had been sent away for the war; but he was certain that, even without Charlie, Benjamin would be capable of considerable mischief.

But perhaps Benjamin was about to confess it all.

"Well?" prompted Mr Mustardpot.

"It's difficult to say," said Benjamin hesitantly.

"Is it about the security breach, about the spy?" asked Mr Mustardpot bluntly.

Benjamin nodded.

"Then I'm afraid your duty is to tell everything you know, Wright," said Mr Mustardpot. "This is a very serious matter. We need all the information we can get to resolve it."

"That's what I thought, sir."

Mr Mustardpot scrutinised the boy sitting in front of him. Apart from Benjamin Wright's great love of pranks and mischief, which often got him into trouble, he was, as far as Mr Mustardpot knew, a kind, fair-minded boy who was very popular with the other children at school. Benjamin wasn't a Christian though, and Mr Mustardpot knew this might lead him into danger, even when Benjamin wasn't aware of any danger at all. Had he even made friends with the spy, and inadvertently led him underground?

"Tell me everything you can," said Mr Mustardpot.

"Well," began Benjamin, "I don't want to land anyone in

trouble, and he is quite a nice old man, but I think I know who the spy is."

"You do?" asked Mr Mustardpot, astonished again at the unexpected turns the interview was taking.

"It's Mr Dim View."

It was certainly the day for surprises. Mr Mustardpot stared intently at Benjamin. Was it possible this was one of his pranks? But surely even Benjamin wouldn't joke at such a terrible crisis. "Are you serious, Wright?" he asked in his most formidable tone.

Benjamin looked surprised – and a little hurt too. "Of course I am," he said. "I wouldn't joke about this, sir!"

"Very well," said Mr Mustardpot. "And have you told anyone else your concerns about, uh, Mr View?"

"No, sir."

"Very well," said Mr Mustardpot again. "And can you tell me why you suspect Mr View of being the betrayer of Aletheia?"

"Well, he's been behaving very oddly, sir," began Benjamin. "I mean, more oddly than usual."

"In what way does this *oddness* manifest itself?" asked Mr Mustardpot.

"He's very nervous, and sneaky…"

"Sneaky?"

"I mean, sneaking glances at everyone and everything, anxious and on edge, and he *does* keep talking about spies!"

"Has it occurred to you, Wright, that Mr View might be concerned about the spy that's rumoured to be hiding near the Food Distribution Centre?"

"No," said Benjamin frankly, "that hadn't occurred to me."

"And, now that it does, could that be a plausible explanation of Mr View's, uh, *odd* behaviour?"

"No," said Benjamin again, "it's far too odd for that!"

Mr Mustardpot sighed. "Have you any other evidence against Mr View, Wright?" he asked.

Benjamin had the sudden, sinking feeling that Mr Mustardpot wasn't taking his concerns about Dim View seriously. He wasn't often angry, but he was annoyed now. Why didn't anyone give him the chance to do anything worthwhile? And now they wouldn't even believe him when he was trying to be helpful about the spy! "I don't have any other, uh, evidence about Mr View," he admitted.

"Look, Wright," said Mr Mustardpot, seeing very clearly that Benjamin was angry and annoyed. "I'll follow up on your information. But in the meantime, can you tell me where you were on the afternoon of the 19th of October, which is two weeks ago, when you had a couple of free hours, when the Distribution Centre was closed for stock-taking?"

"Is that when the spying started?" asked Benjamin. For the moment he couldn't remember what he was doing at the time.

"What were you doing?" asked Mr Mustardpot.

"I can't remember, sir," said Benjamin honestly. "But if that's when the spying started, or the food was poisoned or whatever, then I think I'm right!"

"You're right?" asked the Headmaster.

"Right about Mr View!" said Benjamin. "You see, if the Food Distribution Centre was closed, then Mr View wasn't accounted for! It was when he started the sabotage, you see?"

CHAPTER 26
CATCHING THE SPY

Benjamin pondered his conversation with Mr Mustardpot on his way home after his shift at the Food Distribution Centre. On the whole, he thought that the discussion had gone reasonably well, although he was angry that Mr Mustardpot hadn't taken his theory about Dim View too seriously. And Mr Mustardpot insisted that he wanted him to remember exactly where he was on the 19th of October: it seemed to be important. "I wonder why," mused Benjamin.

Just then, he spotted Mr Cozen, slumbering quietly on a bench which was placed at the corner of a small side street. He had seen Con Cozen a few times since he joined underground Aletheia. He was never doing much; Benjamin assumed the folk at Run-the-Race Retirement Home deemed him too frail and feeble, or too crazy, to work. Often he was dozing somewhere on Benjamin's route home. Usually he was asleep and unresponsive to any of his greetings. But, seeing him now, Benjamin remembered.

That was what he was doing in his spare time on the 19th of October!

He had rescued old Con Cozen from aboveground Aletheia!

Well, here was a dilemma. Benjamin prided himself on being honest and he was sincerely glad he hadn't remembered his whereabouts when he was talking to Mr Mustardpot. How was he going to explain this, without admitting he had been aboveground without permission? He decided he would merely take all reasonable measures to avoid Mr Mustardpot until the Headmaster had forgotten about the matter. It was rather optimistic to hope for this, though: Mr Mustardpot had never forgotten anything like this before. But perhaps the spy would soon be caught. Then Mr Mustardpot wouldn't worry about the 19th of October anymore.

Benjamin considered the matter as he continued through the underground streets on his journey home. There was only one thing to do. Firmly convinced that Dim View was connected to the spying affair, he would simply have to catch him. Then the whole matter would be settled and he would have done something really important for underground Aletheia.

And so Benjamin began to spy on Dim View.

Mr Mustardpot and Mr Straw took the matter of catching the spy who was attacking the food supplies very seriously indeed. Mr Mustardpot begged the privilege of being allowed to coordinate the trap they hoped to lay, and the Management Meeting agreed. He conferred with Mr Straw, and, after the Food Distribution Centre closed that night, they took stock of the piles of potatoes, the crates of apples and pears, the boxes of carrots and leeks, the racks of large cauliflowers, and all the other fruit and vegetables that were organised around the huge Distribution Centre.

"Someone very small could hide in the storage space behind the beans," said Mr Mustardpot. Behind the heap of green beans there was a cupboard. It was well concealed, but it was high enough to see over the main floor area of the Distribution Centre. It wasn't used for much because no one could get at it very easily. But there was a compact hatch in the side of it, and someone small could climb through and keep watch.

"It would serve very well until we can get our traps and other hiding places constructed," said Mr Straw.

"But it's small," said Mr Mustardpot. "That's the snag."

Mr Straw smiled. "If we're looking for two small guards, I think I know just the ones," he said.

Zek and Jack received their instructions soberly and listened earnestly to everything Mr Mustardpot and Mr Straw said to them. They tried not to feel too excited that they had been granted this very special honour of spying on the spy. No one else was delighted at this most trying time, and that very evening the boys overheard Mr Wallop commenting that the Reform Aletheia Competition was rumoured to have been won. And *that* meant *someone* knew how to get to underground Aletheia! But, all the same, it was hard not to feel especially pleased they were chosen for *secret* guard duty that very night.

Apart from Mr and Mrs Wallop, who had given their permission for the venture, they promised not to tell a soul. They bumped into Benjamin on their way to the Centre but, unusually, Benjamin seemed busy with business of his own and he didn't even ask what they were doing. Both boys breathed a sigh of relief. They must keep their secret.

They were undismayed at their not-so-salubrious quarters, squashed in a small cupboard behind a heap of green beans. Neither of them liked green beans, but if that was their hiding place, they were not complaining.

"You're sure you know what to do if you spot something?" asked Mr Straw one final time, before he prepared to leave them for the night watch.

"Yes," called Zek, his voice muffled from inside the cupboard. Small holes had been drilled in the cupboard door. They could see different areas of the Distribution Centre, and just now they could see the large figures of Mr Mustardpot and Mr Straw looking at their cupboard.

"We'll be very close by all night," said Mr Mustardpot. "If you so much as sniff a spy, then you whisper 'Spy' in the Remote Talker!"

"We will," promised Jack.

The footsteps of Mr Mustardpot and Mr Straw faded from the large warehouse. The light around them dimmed for the night.

The two boys crouched in the cupboard and prepared to watch.

It was still and quiet for a long time. Zek dozed quietly, his head nodding backwards and forwards as Jack kept watch. Soon Jack would wake him and they would swap places. They both thought it would be easy to stay awake through the hours of the night, but the excitement quickly wore away and sleepiness overtook them. Jack was about to wake Zek when he noticed a shadow against the heap of potatoes on the opposite side of the Centre. Following the shadow came the substance – in the form of an extremely weird figure which appeared to be camouflaged as…was it possible the person was camouflaged as a cauliflower?! Certainly the person – a man – was in dirty white clothes, with bits of cauliflower stuck out of his ears and one large cauliflower leaf actually perched on his head. Jack stared in disbelief through the small hole. There was only one person he knew who would appear like that, and when the man came closer and pushed and shoved his way behind the racks of cauliflowers, he knew instantly who it was.

It was Dim View!

"Zek!" whispered Jack urgently. "Zek! Wake up!"

Zek opened his eyes and rubbed them sleepily.

"The spy!" Jack hissed quietly. "It's Dim View!"

Instantly Zek was alert. He crouched beside Jack, his eye to the hole in the cupboard.

"He's hidden behind the cauliflowers!" said Jack.

"Are you *sure* it's Dim View?" asked Zek.

"It was him, alright," said Jack, hardly able to understand what he had seen. Why would nice, odd, Mr View be poisoning the supplies of Aletheia?

"What's he hidden for?" asked Zek.

Jack considered that for the first time. Why would the spy, the traitor who was ruining the food, want to hide?

"I know!" he whispered. "I know! It's Dim View, but I bet he's spying on the spy, the same as we are! We'd better not call Mr Mustardpot and Mr Straw until we're sure!"

Zek suddenly clutched his arm. "Jack!" he hissed. "Another spy!"

Both boys were glued to the holes in the cupboard, watching as another long shadow, cast by someone else, crept into the Distribution Centre and quickly vanished behind the pile of potatoes.

In the dim light, in the stillness, Jack and Zek looked at each other, too astonished to speak. It was Benjamin Wright!

"I think," Jack said slowly, "that Ben is following Mr View. Perhaps he thinks he's the spy!"

It was the most logical explanation. For surely Ben couldn't be the spy! And the two newcomers, who now also kept vigil in the large warehouse, certainly weren't poisoning the food. They were watching and waiting too.

The Centre once more settled to uncanny silence. It was weird keeping watch from the cupboard knowing there were other watchers too. Zek and Jack wished they could call to Benjamin, but they did not dare. They both had an eerie feeling something else was afoot.

They did not have long to wait.

Through the utter stillness of night in underground Aletheia came the sound of muffled footsteps. They were cautious, quiet, barely discernible. Then the shadow of the third person to visit the Centre that night came into view.

To Jack and Zek's astonishment it was another old man. He walked quickly but awkwardly, as if walking wasn't quite natural for him, and, apparently not suspecting that anything at all was amiss in the Centre, he immediately made his way to the 'pears' section and extracted a syringe and a needle from his pocket. The two boys were so mesmerised by the sight they just sat and watched the performance as the old man took a vial of green–tinged liquid and filled the syringe.

Then he reached for a pear.

"EEE-WWW-OOO!!"

There was a shriek of incomprehensible fury and Dim View sprang through the cauliflowers, knocking them hither and thither, and leapt for the other old man. In his hand was his large, battered Bible which never left his side, and the light of it suddenly shone dazzlingly through the massive warehouse space, lighting the darkest corners. It fell full on the face of the other old man too. Neither Jack nor Zek recognised him in the first moment of full revelation, but then the strangest, most terrifying thing happened.

In the light of the Bible, the man – the spy who was about to poison the pears – recoiled in terror. And before their very eyes, to the astonishment of them all, he began to change.

It was horrible to see. The shape of the old man began to writhe and twist and turn in grotesque distortions and shapes, accompanied by guttural groaning and hissing. The arms shrank into the body; the legs merged into one; the head pushed downwards into the body, and what was left was a very long, very angry, very large snake!

At some point during the horrifying display, Jack grabbed the Remote Talker. "Spy!" he said urgently. "Spy!" He didn't know if he whispered it or not. It didn't seem to matter now.

The snake-like creature rose high above old Dim View, its slit eyes glowing red and showing hatred. "Youss wills diesss!" it hissed.

The old man beneath the creature, covered in bits of cauliflowers, his eyes large and terrified behind his too-big glasses, held his Bible high. "D-do y-your worst!" he stuttered. "T-there is nothing the Word of God can't protect m-me from!"

"Alethiess wills falls!" hissed the snake. It was going to strike the old man!

Instantly Zek and Jack grabbed their own Bibles. Jack tucked the Remote Talker in his pocket and they clambered from their shelter, rolling down the slope of beans. Neither of them wanted to face the spy that had actually *turned into a snake*, but leaving brave Mr View to face it alone was not an option.

If a snake can appear surprised then this one did. When it caught sight of the two boys, with their Bibles spilling light around them, it began to slither swiftly away. It could not withstand the power of the Word of God. Dim View, moving with more speed than seemed possible, scampered after the creature. Zek and Jack hesitated. They turned as one to the heap of potatoes.

"Ben?" asked Zek uncertainly. "Ben? Are you there?"

CHAPTER 27
FLIGHT THROUGH REDEMPTION SQUARE

White and shaken, Benjamin appeared from behind the potatoes and joined the two smaller boys.

"Are you alright, Ben?" asked Zek. "What are you doing here?"

"W-watching," said Benjamin.

"We were watching too," said Zek. "We sounded the alarm! Mr Mustardpot and Mr Straw should be here soon, and then I expect they'll go after that-that snake thing. Wasn't Dim View so brave?"

But on hearing Mr Mustardpot's name, Benjamin's expression crumpled completely. "What have I done?" he said, his voice catching on a sob. "Whatever have I done?!"

"You, Ben?" asked Zek. "What have you done?"

"I betrayed Aletheia!" said Benjamin wildly, the tears beginning to run down his cheeks. "You don't understand! That old man, that creature, that *thing*, I brought it into underground Aletheia!"

"Are you-are you sure?" asked Zek.

"Of course I'm sure!" said Benjamin.

Quick footsteps, many of them, were coming their way. "Don't tell them I'm here!" whispered Benjamin frantically. "Don't give me away!"

He once more vanished behind the potatoes, just as Mr Mustardpot, at the head of a considerable army of Rescuers, rushed into the Centre.

"Which way, boys?" boomed the Headmaster.

"They went that way!" said Jack quickly, pointing to one of the exits. "Follow the bits of cauliflower!" Whether or not Mr View cleverly intended it, there were certainly small, white sprinklings of cauliflower marking the direction in which he followed the spy.

Mr Mustardpot didn't hesitate or ask pointless questions about the cauliflower. He plunged through the exit, the Rescuers following him, and soon the warehouse was empty once more.

"Ben?" Zek called uncertainly. "Ben? What are you going to do?"

Benjamin rejoined them. He seemed incapable of deciding anything. "I wish I was dead!" he said miserably.

Jack, with a cooler head, said, "Let's at least go after them and see what happens. It might turn out alright for you, Ben." He didn't know that, of course, but at least it was a plan of action.

They tailed along at the rear of the group of hurrying Rescuers. Now and again, Jack saw a small, white sprinkling of cauliflower marking the way. But it was not hard, after all, to figure out where the snake-spy had gone. They were headed for the source of the Water of Sound Doctrine.

The angry shrieks and hisses of the snake were terrific when the forces of Aletheia converged on it. Mr Mustardpot's Rescuers pursued from the rear, and Mr Sturdy Wright's Rescuers, who were protecting and defending the precious Water of Sound Doctrine, attacked from the front. In one last attempt to poison the source, the snake had attempted to fling itself into the middle of the sparkling reservoir of water. But Sturdy Wright's forces threw themselves on the creature, sending it backwards under the fierce light of their Bibles. They quickly produced ropes and hooks and an assortment of other things with which they attempted to trap it.

"Youss aress doomsss!" hissed the snake.

"You are doomed!" cried Mr Straw, a pitchfork in one hand, a Bible in the other. "Who are you, the filth of Err, that dares to attack the Truth?!"

The snake shrieked and hissed and writhed as it rose, and recoiled, and tried to strike its many opponents with its sharp, poisonous fangs. But the light of the Bible was in its eyes and it could not see.

"Who let you in?" thundered Mr Mustardpot, now in the thick of the fight.

The snake peered down at the Headmaster with strange, intelligent delight in its cruel, red eyes. "Benjaminss Wrightsss!" it hissed with evident relish.

There was a cry of dismay from Sturdy Wright as he fell to the ground. The Rescuers close to him gathered him up and others took his place.

And, as the fight to contain the snake continued, as they tied their knots and cast their nets around it, Benjamin fled. He ran as fast as he could run.

In terror and shame.

In abject misery.

He ran away.

"Ben, wait!" cried Zek, as he and Jack began to run after him. "Wait!"

And then there was no breath to say more. It was a good job Jack Merryweather was such a fast runner, and even he found it hard to keep up. He pounded after Benjamin through the underground entry leading to the Academy of Soldiers-of-the-Cross, through the corridors, around countless twists and turns, until suddenly Benjamin stopped. He was standing by a small, external Bible-access-only door which led onto the aboveground streets of Aletheia. There was no sign of Zek. They had lost him somewhere along the way. There was only Jack and Benjamin.

"Help me, please, Jack," he said miserably. "Let me out!"

Jack fingered the Bible which was warm and reassuring in his hand. "Where do you want to go?" he asked.

"I need to go to Justification," said Benjamin. "I *must go!*"

Jack simply nodded. He did not think of the obstacles in the way. He could not think of anything better for Benjamin than, at last, understanding how to be cleared of every guilty charge. This was Ben's greatest need. He placed the Bible in the book-shaped indentation on the door, and the catch released with a gentle click.

Benjamin began to run again, onto the dark streets of Aletheia. But this time he did not seem to mind that Jack was running with him.

Once again it was raining in the city. There were holes and gaps in the streets where the workers of Err were 'improving' it. They ran around machinery and vehicles now parked at the side of the road. But there were no people about in the middle of the night.

When they stood at the edge of Redemption Square, they looked across the sea of protesters who were sleeping inside their tents and huts. A few were awake, though; and more were emerging from their shelters. There was a feeling of dismay, of disarray, among them, and, as crazy as the idea seemed, Jack wondered whether there was an invisible link between them and the defeat of the snake beneath the ground. Benjamin hesitated at the edge of the square. Jack held his Bible in his hand and watched as warm, golden rays spilled from it onto the shining, wet paving slabs of the square. "We'll follow the light of the Bible," he said firmly. "We'll be alright then."

Benjamin didn't question this. He followed in Jack's footsteps, threading his way through the large, messy, disorganised campsite, past the people who were rubbing their eyes and asking their friends what was wrong. Jack hesitated when they reached the cross. This spot, at the foot of the cross, always felt like the safest place in the land. He had thought that nothing could meddle with the cross. But was it any less safe now, despite the fact they were surrounded by the foes of Err? Strangely, he didn't think so. The cross was still standing.

The Truth was not changed, no matter how much people wanted to believe otherwise.

"People used to say nothing could change the Truth of the cross,"[12] said Benjamin. He sounded weary now; as if he was almost out of hope. "But look at the protesters."

"Yes, camping out in the rain!" exclaimed Jack. "They can't even get into the buildings of Truth around the square! And don't you see how worried they are?"

A large man shambled towards them, looking in their direction, as if he could hear their conversation. Jack held his Bible high above him and Benjamin. The man walked past blankly, as if he could not see them at all. Perhaps he could not. The light of the Bible was like a blanket around them, making them invisible to their enemies. They continued through the quickly waking square, through the protesters who, even when awake, seemed unaware of them. At last they reached the building of Justification. It was silent, but Jack knew there were guards beyond the pillars, defending the Truth. He walked up the steps, followed by Benjamin. He wondered how they would get in.

Hugo and Timmy, two of a team of Rescuers guarding Justification that night, stood quietly behind the pillars, hardly able to believe their eyes. If they weren't completely mad, or perhaps dreaming, the two figures threading their way through the square were Jack Merryweather and Benjamin Wright! They could easily see the light of Jack's Bible; they knew some adventure, or misadventure, lay behind this night excursion across Redemption Square. They stood back to watch as both boys clambered up the steps. Jack, they knew, could enter. He was a Christian and carried his Bible. But Benjamin…?

Benjamin stumbled. It felt like he had hit a brick wall! Jack had vanished into Justification but Benjamin could see nothing but darkness ahead of him. Tears began to fall down his cheeks once more. He was doomed. He could not even enter into Justification.

"Ben?" Faint but nearby, it was Hugo's voice, which came from behind the pillars of Justification.

"Hugo?" Benjamin pressed forward, as far as he dared, squinting into the pillars. Behind him, the large man who blindly passed them at the foot of the cross, and a couple of other people too, were coming to Justification, curious about the boy they could now clearly see.

"We need to ask you a pass question, Ben," said Hugo. "Then you can get in."

"Quickly, please!" begged Benjamin.

The man began to climb the steps. "Who are you talking to, boy?" he demanded. "Do you know how to get in?"

"How can man be justified with God?" asked Hugo.

"Someone's talking!" exclaimed the man. "There's someone inside this building!"

"Through the Lord Jesus!" cried Benjamin. He had been taught that answer all his life; but never had his life depended on it as it did now.

"Quick, Ben!" said Hugo, and Benjamin took a single bound up the steps and was pulled quickly through the pillars by Hugo and Timmy.

The man on the steps outside gave a loud shout. "He's got in! There's a way in!" he yelled. Dozens of people began to emerge from shelters, dishevelled but excited. They began to pound across the square to the steps of Justification, converging there as Hugo and Timmy cried for reinforcements.

"Jack, take Ben inside," said Hugo, as more senior Rescuers began to take their stand by the pillars. "We're needed here!" He and Timmy took their places with them. They only hoped they hadn't just jeopardised underground Aletheia.

"The answer to the question is 'Jesus'!" shouted the man who overheard Benjamin's response.

But Justification was unyielding. The man did not believe what he was saying. Someone in the crowd lifted a stone and sent it flying into Justification. Timmy quickly lifted his Bible to block it and the stone spun crazily away again, hitting one of the crowd on the head. Jack and Benjamin left the shouts behind.

Jack led the way into the courtroom of Justification.

CHAPTER 28
WEIGHED IN THE BALANCES

Jack had seen the courtroom of Justification before. It was a frightening and awesome room. In the centre, before the high and exalted judge's seat, there was a ghastly hole. It was dark and deep and went a long, long way down. Perhaps it never stopped. Perhaps it led to another place entirely. From the hole emerged a long metal pole that supported a high beam, from which hung a huge pair of metal plates. These were the balances that measured whether or not a person was right before God.

Jack was not afraid of the balances. He had trusted in the Lord Jesus to pay the debt he owed to God for all his sins. He could stand on the scales and know that they would not lower into the darkness with the weight of his sin, because God had taken it all away. Benjamin, however, had never trusted in the Lord Jesus. Jack knew that Ben should not stand on the balances without relying on Him to pay the price God's justice demanded. If he did, he would be doomed!

Benjamin hesitated at the sight of the courtroom before them. An arrow indicated the way to one of the metal plates which hung from the high beam. White and tense, he hurried to the balance. He didn't stop to read the instructions about how to be justified, or the warning about what would happen if you were found wanting. He just wanted to understand the Truth at last. Justification. Old Dim View said it was something to do with Justification! The answer must be here.

"Ben! Wait!" cried Jack. "It's too dangerous! You can't get on the balances…!"

"I've got to find out!" said Benjamin. "I've got to find the Truth! I thought I was alright, you see? But I couldn't even see the lies of Con Cozen because I didn't know the Truth! Even Dim View could see what he was, but I was blind!"

Jack, who didn't even know who Con Cozen was, said nothing. He only knew that Benjamin needed to understand the Truth of the message of salvation and be made right before God. "Ben, you need the Lord Jesus to pay…!"

But Benjamin had already stepped across the narrow bridge that led onto the balance, trying not to look over the edge: he didn't want to think how far away the bottom of the hole was, or where it went to. When he stepped onto the balance, the bridge silently retracted and vanished; now there was no way back.

For a moment the balances did nothing at all. They were level and steady, as if silently assessing the situation. And then a strange thing happened. To Benjamin's awful dismay and embarrassment, the balance on which he stood began to fill with all the wrong things of his past. Every single wrong thing he had ever said or thought or done was represented by horrible pointy, prickly, uncomfortable weights. He didn't know where they came from, but they were plinking and plonking onto the balance with him, one horrible wrong after another. It was awful to realise that there were so many. The scales soon began to tip, and he began to sink on the balance, tilting precariously over the terrifying black hole, clinging desperately to his perch which was lowering and lowering and lowering...always downwards...

Soft, fluffy clouds of good things settled on the other side of the balance, not making the slightest difference. Benjamin's kindness, his honesty, his hard work at the Food Distribution Centre – all these things were represented there. They looked nice, but they weighed nothing at all. Not all the good deeds that he had done would ever alter the balance in his favour. They could not make payment for sin.

Down towards the depths of darkness he went.

As he sank he noticed writing flashing ominously from the judge's bench. 'Guilty! Guilty! Guilty!' flashed in bold black writing, again and again and again.

Benjamin's mind was full of dread. At any moment he might vanish into the darkness beneath him. But he knew that before God he was indeed guilty of wrong. The Bible said everyone had fallen short of

God's standards[15]. There was no defence. People were all helpless and hopeless sinners.

Jack watched the scene in horror. "No!" he shouted, as Benjamin continued to sink. Bravely, he leaned over the edge of the hole, trying to reach for the opposite balance which was rising as Benjamin went down. "I can't pull it down, Ben!" Jack sobbed, beside himself for his friend. "No-one can! You must trust in the Lord Jesus to pay the price for you!"

'Death sentence!' was the next awful statement which flashed, in blood-red this time, from the judge's bench. 'Death! Death! Death!'

"Help!" cried Benjamin. "What shall I do?" Tears poured down his cheeks. He knew it was all true. He had nothing to offer God as payment for his sins.

"Believe on the Lord Jesus!" called Jack again. "It's the blood which He shed at the cross which will remove all your sins!"

And, in desperation, Benjamin did exactly that. He had already come to the conclusion that he needed something other than himself to trust in. He had messed up so badly with his good intentions, even to the point of betraying Aletheia. The others were right all along. It was not the Bible that was lacking or useless, it was his trust, his confidence in it, which was at fault. And so Benjamin cried to God that He believed in the Lord Jesus and wanted Him to pay the price for his sins…

Suddenly, just in time to stop Ben vanishing entirely into the darkness below, there was an altogether different message from the judge's bench. In bright, radiant light, high above the seat, shining and glowing unmistakably, were the words, 'Paid! Paid! Paid!'

The balance began to rise steadily. The awful, heavy weights of sins vanished completely from the side on which Benjamin stood, and on the opposite dish, where once there were the good things Ben had done, which made absolutely no difference to his predicament, there was the glimmer of precious blood. The scales didn't stop when they were level again; Ben's side of the balance went on rising, taking him up to the high level of the judge's seat – whilst the balance containing blood went deeper and deeper into the abyss below.

A narrow bridge unfolded, leading from the high plate on which Ben stood to the judge's bench itself. Benjamin walked across it, onto the cushioned, velvet richness of the high bench. He looked down in silence on Jack who was watching the scene in astonishment.

In clear gold writing across the wall behind the judge's bench was now written, 'Just, and the Justifier of those who believe in Jesus'[17]. The messages of guilt and death had been about Ben; but this message was all about God, and what He had done to make Ben right, when he trusted in the Lord Jesus.

Benjamin descended from the judge's seat, and silently the balances returned to level over the gaping hole.

"I don't know what it all means," said Ben in awe, "but I know God has done right for me when I couldn't do it myself!"

"It's because you've trusted in the Lord Jesus," said Jack. "*That's* what made the difference on the balances! It's the Lord Jesus who allows God to be both Just, and the Justifier."

For the first time, Benjamin realised what it meant. God was Just: He must demand proper payment for sin[15], as any righteous judge would do; and He was the Justifier: because He provided the full payment Himself, through the death and shedding of blood of the Lord Jesus. It had been awful to realise he was doomed because of all the wrong things he had done. But it was wonderful to know, because he had trusted in the Lord Jesus, God cleared Ben of every single charge[14].

For anyone who trusted in the Lord Jesus, God so completely blotted out their sins, it was as if they had never sinned at all!

As they left the courtroom scene, words in gold shone from the door. The words said, 'Justification: Declared Righteous'.

That was the secret of Justification. It made people right with God.

"I think I know now why there are so many guards protecting Justification," said Jack slowly as they left the courtroom. "Some people think that you can pay for forgiveness in gold, but there's only one payment God will accept for sin. Money, and gold crosses, and good things, and other stuff won't work on the balances – only the blood of the Lord Jesus can do that."

Benjamin nodded. "I'm really and truly fit for Heaven!" he exclaimed. He was so happy that his wrongdoings had been cleared away by God – all because of what the Lord Jesus had done. "But I wonder if I'm fit for facing my father," he added ruefully.

Jack didn't know what to say to comfort him. Benjamin was now a Christian. But in these first few glad moments he must put right the wrong he had done.

Benjamin must now face his Headmaster and his father.

CHAPTER 29
STRIKE BACK

Zek was waiting for Jack and Ben at the underground entry point into Justification, through which the two boys re-joined underground Aletheia.

"You look much better, Ben!" he exclaimed.

"I'm saved, Zek!" said Benjamin, the shine of happiness and relief unmistakable on his face. "God cleared all my sin away! There's nothing I can be judged for now!"

"How did you know we'd be here, Zek?" Jack asked curiously.

"I knew you'd gone to Justification, and thought you would come back through here," Zek explained. "Hugo and Timmy let Bourne know what happened and about you arriving at Justification. There was a fight at the front of Justification too! So everyone knows where you went. And Dusty alerted Bourne that someone left the Academy through the same door that was breached on the 19th of October – I don't know why the date is important but they seem to think it is – and so they realised that's the route you and Jack took."

Benjamin sighed. "Do you know where my father is?" he asked Zek.

"Uncle Sturdy is in an emergency Management Meeting with the rest of the managers," he said.

Bravely, Ben squared his shoulders. "Then that's where I've got to go," he said.

For once, those gathered for the Management Meeting were not dressed in neat, pressed uniforms, and crisp, clean shirts. Instead, they had the appearance of people who had rushed helter-skelter just to be there. Some had not even been to bed that long night. Mr Straw was one of these. He had dressed in old dungarees and armed himself with farming implements and his Bible, keeping watch close by the Food Distribution Centre with his friend, Philologus Mustardpot. Since then, he had chased and fought a huge, angry snake: so it was not to be wondered at that he stood in front of the important people of Aletheia in stained, torn overalls, his hair sticking out at all angles, with a pitchfork behind his chair because he had forgotten to put it away.

Nobody minded. There was too much at stake to care about how people were dressed.

"The wretched creature is contained in the dungeons, under guard?" asked the Chief.

"Yes, Chief," said Mr Straw.

"And we're certain he wasn't working with anyone else?"

Mr Straw hesitated. "No one else remains a threat, Chief," he said.

The name of Benjamin Wright had already reverberated around the room. He did not wish to add to the burdens of distraught Sturdy Wright by another mention of the boy's connection with the creature. Poor Sturdy Wright sat with his head in his hands. But he and his guards had proved heroic that night. Not one drop of snake-venom polluted the underground source of the Water of Sound Doctrine.

"Theo, I know it's early days, but, from your brief examination of our captive, what do you think we're dealing with here?"

Dr Theo Pentone rose to his feet. He had tartan slippers on his feet and was clothed in his dressing gown, over which was a stained lab coat. He did not seem in the least bit concerned by his attire. "I believe the creature is a Deceivedor created by the Academy of Science-Explains-All," said Dr Pentone. "The description of the creature's shape-changing ability, the fact it cannot keep up its deception in the light of the Bible, and its current form and shape as a snake, all lead me to believe that that is probably what it is. The creation of these types of creatures is quite new technology for Err and the Academy of Science-Explains-All, and never, to my knowledge, have they been used in this way before. Frankly, they must have been desperate to try it!"

The Chief nodded. "I suspected as much," he said.

"Although I'm somewhat surprised this creature was acting on its own," added Dr Pentone. "We had intelligence that Err had developed dozens of these beasts. I would have assumed there would be a number of them working together!"

"Then we can be thankful only one Deceivedor reached us," said the Chief.

"Rescuers have been working all night scouring the underground for any sign of further creatures, but we're certain this one was alone," added Captain Steadfast.

Hardy Wallop suspected he knew why only one Deceivedor had reached underground Aletheia. He was convinced that Jack's brother, who he pictured as strong and capable and fearless, had somehow kept the others away.

"On another matter, which is possibly linked to the Deceivedor, Outpost Rescuer Markerpen has, in the last hour, informed me that the winner of the Reform Aletheia Competition is going to be publicly announced tomorrow," said the Chief. "The Council of Err is confident they have not only found our hiding place, but can access it too."

"We think it's likely they will try to gain access through Door Nineteen," Captain Steadfast continued. "This is where the snake, Con Cozen, entered. But it's possible that the plans of the Council of Err rely on Con Cozen still being present and active. They're probably not yet aware that the creature is now a captive."

"Are we ready to take back our city, Captain?" asked the Chief formally of his son.

"I believe we are ready to take back the city, sir," replied Captain Steadfast. "Our attack scenarios have been worked through, our forces are on standby."

"I say we strike soon!" said Philologus Mustardpot. "It seems to me we must move before our enemy realises their spy has been caught. We don't know the creature's communication methods, or when they might realise the game is up!"

"I think I recall, from my limited study of Deceivedors, that they are programmed with a signal which is emitted frequently to the owner," explained Dr Pentone. "On changing into the snake, it's possible the Deceivedor already gave a signal of defeat to the Council of Err."

"I think time is of the essence," said Chief Judge Steady.

"I agree," said Hardy Wallop.

"Then, if our prayer cover is good enough, we should strike back at first light in the morning," agreed the Chief.

Captain Steadfast hastily left the room to prepare his troops.

"All the rest of you know your duties. Do them well!"

It was then, as they gathered their papers together and Mr Straw sheepishly picked up his pitchfork, that there was a timid knock on the door.

"Come in," commanded the Chief.

In walked Benjamin Wright, unwitting betrayer of Aletheia, to face the assembled company. "I've come to explain," he said.

CHAPTER 30
ALL GO!

There was an eerie hush across underground Aletheia. Hardly anyone was at work. No one attended the Food Distribution Centre. No one swept the underground streets, or watered the tubs of flowers. The cattle and other animals were fed for the day, but no one watched over them now. Everyone who was not part of the mighty fighting force which stood clustered at the exits into Aletheia, was praying.

Never mind breakfast.

Never mind other duties.

The future of Aletheia was at stake!

It was still early in the morning. Some people had not even gone to bed. Mr Mustardpot and Mr Straw and Jack and Zek were among these, but no one thought about being tired. Not today.

Dusty was at work. He would not leave the Central Control Room in the Academy of Soldiers-of-the-Cross until aboveground Aletheia was once more in the hands of the defenders of the Truth. Many of the staff of the Control Room had volunteered for the fight, and new volunteers were drafted in to watch the machines and shout the readings to Dusty and Mr Buffer, who would keep the commanders of the battle informed.

Among the newcomers in the Control Room were Zek and Jack and Benjamin. They were too inexperienced to go out to battle so they would watch and guard behind the scenes. When Jack saw the Control Room for the first time, with all its fantastical machines, he couldn't imagine any place he'd rather be. Hector also arrived to 'help' in the Control Room. Dusty was dubious about his presence, but there was, as Zek pointed out, no actual specific rule that forbad it.

Dusty didn't want to disappoint Zek. "Keep him out of Mr Buffer's way," he warned. Mr Buffer, stationed on a high platform to oversee the work of the Control Room, had more than enough to worry about without the disruptive influence of Hector.

Zek, whose role was to watch the Revealer Device, tied Hectors' lead to the legs of the machine and told him to 'stay'. Hector never knew what that meant, but, happily for Zek, the Revealer Device had a fascinating series of wheels which flew round and round at top speed, and Hector was entranced. He sat stock still, ears pricked up, watching the wheels turn, his head going this way and that in a most comic performance. Zek watched him proudly.

"I knew he'd know what to do!" he said.

Despite the fact they were on the brink of battle, the Control Room was a marvel of calm competence. Mr Buffer, who was pale and exhausted from months of overwork, watched everything that was happening and relied on young Dusty Addle, his assistant, to coordinate the work of the volunteers on the floor. Zek and Jack and Ben were very proud of their important friend. Dusty was practically in charge!

Mr Buffer had a special link with Captain Steadfast, who was the battle commander. He communicated with the Captain through a golden tube which twisted and snaked its way into the wall of the Control Room, invisibly continuing its link to Captain Steadfast. "Testing, testing…" Mr Buffer said through the tube.

"Received, Brian." Captain Steadfast's clipped, no-nonsense tone filled the Control Room. In the background, they could hear the final battle preparations being made. There were muffled voices, and the whirl of the Captain's Rescue Capsule engine, and the clatter of machinery and equipment.

Along with several others, Jack and Ben were assigned to watch the massive Central Mission Detector which just now showed all the streets and details of Aletheia. On the screen, the Academy of Soldiers-of-the-Cross was seething with moving coloured dots. Transport vehicles and Rescue Capsules were coded orange; Senior Rescuers were coded red; the remainder of the fighting force were green. And if you raised the long, pointed, silver stick, and hovered over any colour, it showed you exactly who or what it was.

"Wow!" said Benjamin. He lifted the silver pointer and placed it over one of the few white specks in the Control Room of the Academy. "It's you, Jack!" he said. "It actually shows us here too!"

Benjamin was very happy to be included in any task to help the battle for Aletheia. He hadn't thought he deserved to do anything at all, not after he had so nearly ruined everything. But he had learned something remarkable when he had faced the Management Meeting the previous night. He learned that, because God had completely wiped out all his guilt and all the charges anyone could bring against him, the managers and people of Aletheia would do likewise. "They told me the Bible says that God will not remember my sins anymore because of what the Lord Jesus has done,"[18] Benjamin explained to

Jack, as they watched the coloured marks move around the screen. "So they have a policy that, if you've repented of your sins, other Christians shouldn't remember them either! Of course, I've still got things to put right. I've got to apologise to the Rescuer who almost got into trouble because I followed him out of the door. And I must find Mr View and say sorry for falsely accusing him. But..."

Benjamin's words were cut short.

The Aletheia Alert alarm sounded sharply through the Control Room, cutting over the buzz of battle preparations.

Jack and Ben and Zek stayed where they were as they had been instructed. The Control Room *must* stay in order. Hector, who hated the awful screech, hid beneath the Revealer Device.

Dusty hurried to the panicked-looking old man watching the Aletheia Alert device and calmly quieted the alarm. He peered closely at the machine, then lifted a speaking tube and spoke to Mr Buffer. Mr Buffer listened intently to Dusty's message and then spoke into the golden tube link with Captain Steadfast. "Captain Steadfast? Come in, Captain..."

"Received," barked Captain Steadfast, his voice echoing loudly around the Control Room.

"We have an Alert on Door Nineteen of the Academy, sir. Unknown object preparing to penetrate the door."

Dusty joined the others at the Central Mission Detector screen. "Keep an eye on Door Nineteen," he directed.

"Received," said Captain Steadfast briefly. "Status on prayer?"

Mr Buffer looked at the massive Prayer Power Monitor which was stationed in the centre of the Control Room. "Strong...no!" Excitement filled Mr Buffer's usually monotone voice. "We're now on *Abundant*, sir! We're ready to go!"

"That's awesome!" Dusty murmured to Jack. "We didn't know if we'd make it that high!"

"Go!" roared Captain Steadfast's voice, now speaking to the commanders around him. "All go!"

The battle for Aletheia had begun.

CHAPTER 31
THE BATTLE FOR ALETHEIA

Hugo and Timmy took their places in Rescue Capsule Three-Sixteen. They had been granted permission to join the Capsule of which Harold Wallop was the co-pilot. Harold's seat was in the small flight cabin. He was in charge of liaising with the eight occupants, including Hugo and Timmy, in the main cabin of the Rescue Capsule. The two boys gripped the arms of their seats as the marvellous flying machine shot into the air.

Usually the flight of a Capsule was so smooth you could barely feel movement. But this was no ordinary take-off; and this was no ordinary flight. Capsule after Capsule zoomed straight up into the air from the hidden Launch Pad at the top of one of the towers of the Academy of Soldiers-of-the-Cross. They scattered across the sky in precisely the formation that the battle plan required. In a matter of minutes, they were hovering around the boundary of Aletheia, above the polluted Water of Sound Doctrine, surrounding the city in a never ending circle, like all the tiny second marks on a big round clock.

It happened so quickly that the people from Err hardly glimpsed the big round Capsules' flights. They were mostly massed around the Academy, excited and determined to follow the big bulldozer into the fortress through Door Nineteen and find the weird and wonderful things they were certain were within. They all heard the sudden strange whirring of the engines, and a couple of more observant people thought a large flock of birds flew out of a high tower, far above them. But they had no idea the city was now surrounded by the Rescuers of the Academy of Soldiers-of-the-Cross.

Further away from the Academy, the people who remained in camps and fairs on the Pray-Always Farmlands, and those who had moved into the vacated houses in The Outskirts, looked up in awe and horror at the sight. It was still early in the morning; the sun was only now lighting the sky with streaks of gold. Most of the folk on the farmlands were still in bed when the strange whooshing and whirring of the invasion began.

Some were already awake and were trying to revive their campfires and keep warm. There had been a sharp frost in the night; another reminder that winter was not far away. But they had hoped that last night would be the final night they would spend on the farmlands. The Council of Err had promised that today the takeover of the city would be complete. Today they hoped to be moving into the empty buildings and sturdy homes in central Aletheia; they would be out of the awful wet autumn, and warm and snug in the old city before the first snow fell.

But the sight of the round, hovering Capsules, which appeared intent on invading Aletheia, did *not* seem to be part of the Council of Err's plan. They didn't look like the armies of Err at all! To the invaders of the Pray-Always Farmlands they were an awful alien invasion, not the homecoming of the rightful occupants of the city of Bible Truth. And what was the *thing* each Capsule clutched beneath it…?

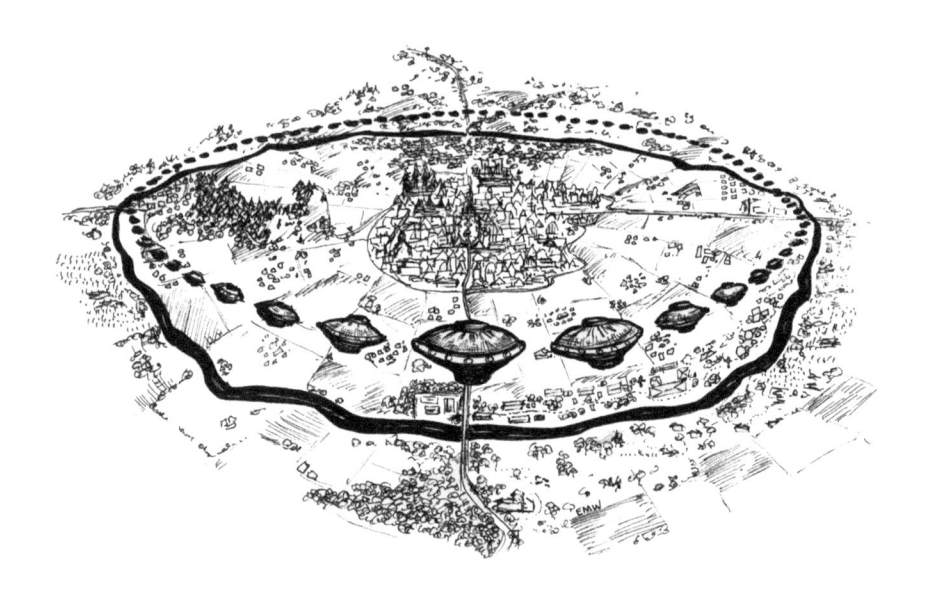

"I wish I could see the expression on their faces," exclaimed Hugo, peering through a round window as Capsule Three-Sixteen, recovered and improved from a previous adventure[10], continued to hover stationary at the edge of Aletheia.

Harold spoke from the co-pilot's seat, "Well, actually, you might be able to. We've replaced the glass in the windows with Spy-Glass, newly developed for the war. Fix on a spot, and then look closely."

Hugo settled on a fixed point, looking into the garden of a home in lavish Take-It-Easy Luxury Housing. As he watched, the garden became clearer and clearer, closer and closer, until he could see the bush that was shaped like a peacock, the bird table, the small robin on the bird table, even the very smallest crumbs on the bird table! "Wow!" he murmured. He looked at the large windows of the luxurious house. A man, in his dressing gown, was enjoying a large mug of coffee and a big wedge of toast. He was holding his drink in one hand and his toast in the other. He was standing at the window, his mouth open in astonishment and fear, and, as Hugo watched, he dropped the china mug and the toast fell limply from his hand. The mug smashed and dark liquid spilled down the window and all over the floor. The man ran from the room. "This will be a nice wake up call for the people in The Outskirts," Hugo mumbled to himself.

"When will it start?" asked Timmy, as the Capsule continued to hover in line with the many others.

"Anytime now," came Harold's voice into the main cabin. "We wait for the Captain's command."

When the Aletheia Alert sounded for Door Nineteen, Benjamin

was determined to guard the door with his eyes. It was, he was certain, the very door through which he had inadvertently betrayed Aletheia. He *must* watch it and try and put right what he had done wrong. He stared fixedly at the door on the map and, when the first blow fell, he gave a startled cry and pointed at the massive Mission Detector screen. "Dusty!" he yelled.

"On my way," said Dusty cheerfully. The orange dots of the Rescue Capsules, all safely in place at exactly the right time, were stationary. It was a strange pattern on the screen. The entire city was now ringed in a protective orange glow. But it was the bright red flashing light at Door Nineteen which caught their attention now.

"Door Nineteen, sir!" Dusty called to Mr Buffer. He didn't need to explain further.

"Captain? Door Nineteen is now insecure. Repeat, breach at Door Nineteen."

"Received!" barked the Captain. It sounded, from the background noises around him, that Captain Steadfast was in one of the Capsules which now encircled the city.

"That's his Capsule there," explained Dusty. "Capsule Rom-Eight-Thirty-Three. He's overseeing the battle from the sky." He pointed to one of the orange marks, the only one with a bright red centre.

"Capsule Three-Sixteen?" came Captain Steadfast's voice.

"Three-Sixteen receiving you, sir," said Harold over the crackle of airwaves.

"Change of plan for you, Three-Sixteen. Assistance needed at Door Nineteen of the Academy. Drop-Strike immediately. Repeat, Drop-Strike immediately."

"Immediately, sir!"

Their Capsule shot forward. Timmy and Hugo gripped their seats. Now the war was truly beginning. And their Capsule would start it!

"Action stations," ordered Harold from the co-pilot's seat, as the Capsule swiftly approached the massive crowd which now clustered around the narrow alleyway leading to Door Nineteen. Small levers popped up around the perimeter of the floor, and the six experienced Rescuers in the main cabin immediately left their seats – although they were still tied by safety cords to their stations – and clustered around the outside of the floor, working the small levers. Hugo and Timmy watched. They were there as backup, to fetch and carry anything the other Rescuers might need. They had no experience of working the mechanics of the fantastic Rescue Capsule.

On the first rapid turn of the lever, the round centre of the floor dropped by several inches; on the second it split neatly into four segments which vanished from sight, folding precisely into the underbelly of the Capsule. A blast of fresh air suddenly filled the cabin. There was now a large hole in the floor, and, directly beneath the Capsule, was a massive tank, filled with the greatest weapon the Rescuers possessed.

"Ready to release cargo, sir," said the most senior of the six Rescuers crouched on the floor.

"On my orders," said Harold. "Targeted Hit only. We'll need additional cargo for other targets."

One Rescuer pressed a series of keys on a compact control panel he extracted from his pocket. There were funnels and chutes and hoses to assist with the release of the weapon and, as the Rescuer pressed control keys, a large funnel swung into place from beneath the Capsule.

Hugo and Timmy could now see the motley crew surrounding Door Nineteen. A huge bulldozer had stuck its ugly metal mouth into the small wooden door through which Benjamin had gone on his adventure. It was raising its massive iron front to strike again when Harold gave the order, "Hit!" and the Capsule released its first drop.

Gallons of pure Water of Sound Doctrine cascaded through the funnel, directly onto the bulldozer of Err and the people surrounding it.

Hugo and Timmy gave a rousing cheer before they thought better of it, but the six Rescuers who were manning the chutes and funnels through which the water was channelled also gave a shout of triumph. And from the front of the Capsule they could distinctly hear the delight of Harold and the pilot too.

The bulldozer was suddenly still and silent: turned to a statue, drenched in water that disabled its engines and functions so it could do no more. The officials of Err who were overseeing the all-important break-through to the Academy cried out in confusion and dismay. This rain storm was nothing like the unpleasant autumn storms the city had been struck with lately. This water fell from a cloudless blue sky. This water stung! They cried out, running backwards into the crowd which blocked the way. "Get undercover!" they yelled. "Toxic water!"

"Door Nineteen cleared, sir," Harold said calmly to his Captain.

"Good work, Wallop," said Captain Steadfast. "I'll let the Control Room know. They can dispatch troops to make a temporary repair. We're ready for Air Rescue now. Standby, and then, since you're in the vicinity, continue your mission at Redemption Square."

"Yes, sir!" said Harold.

"Air Rescue, go!" came the command of the Captain, and within seconds the waiting Rescue Capsules descended in organised formation on their beloved city. Capsule Three-Sixteen shot forward again, but they did not have far to go. They streaked towards Redemption Square, following the crowds of protesters who fled from Door Nineteen and were now stampeding for their tents and shelters in the square.

"Prepare for Big Hit," said Harold.

"Ready, sir."

"Hit!"

And hit they did. Over the centre of the square, over the cross itself, a deluge of the cleansing, purifying water cascaded over the ground below in one triumphant blast. Hugo and Timmy followed the action beneath them. The tents and crude shelters were no match for the Water of Sound Doctrine. It cut through the fabric and wood and plastic and even metal as if they simply weren't there. It washed away the slogans and protest banners as if they had never existed. Materials of all sorts went flying higgledy-piggledy in every direction. Hugo remembered being on guard duty in Justification, watching Redemption Square and wishing it could all be washed clean. He never dreamed then that it was possible: but this was exactly what was happening! And when the tents and shelters were washed away, people cowered wet and wretched on the paving slabs of the square, utterly exposed.

"It burns!" some yelled.

"It stings!" wailed others.

"Toxic!" they cried.

"What burns and stings?" asked Timmy, watching with bewilderment as people began to flee from the centre of the city, trying to escape other water drops from other Capsules – which were now happening on every street.

"They feel the sting of the Water of Sound Doctrine," explained one of the Rescuers briefly. "Permission to hit Election Terrace, sir?"

"Permission granted," said Harold.

The Rescuer aimed a funnel at the row of extremely ancient cottages on which was written a protest slogan. It was a direct hit and the other Rescuers cheered as the water washed the wall of the cottage clean and sent the letters of the slogan helter-skelter down the drain.

"Why does the water sting the people?" pursued Timmy.

"Because they don't believe the Truth of the Bible," said a Rescuer. "It's always painful to be hit by the Truth when you won't believe!"

Timmy thought about that as they continued to watch the masses flee from Aletheia because they could not stand the Truth of the Word of God. He remembered that when he had first come to Aletheia he had hated the sight of the Water of Sound Doctrine. Timmy wasn't a Christian then, and, to him, the water was dirty and unpalatable[2].

This was the effect it had on those who did not believe, who could not bear to face up to what the Word of God said about them, and who missed out on all the marvellous things God had in store for people who believed. It was why the water was the best protection the city could have – until the Meddlers polluted it. But today even that would be put right, and pure Water of Sound Doctrine would once more flow around the city of Truth.

Strangely, one or two people from Err – only a very few – did not flee with the rest. They looked surprised at the drenching water. They were dazed and puzzled. But they did not seem to feel it sting and bite as others did. And when Capsule Three-Sixteen left Redemption Square fully cleansed of defilement, and went to re-fill with water and continue the battle elsewhere, there was one girl who remained and was now sitting on the steps, at the foot of the cross.

She was the girl with purple hair who had once looked for the hidden people of Aletheia – and had followed Hugo and Timmy across the Pray-Always Farmlands.

Crystal had come to the cross.

CHAPTER 32
THE OUTCOME

Across central Aletheia, and across the vast Pray-Always Farmlands, similar scenes were taking place. Hit after hit, drop after drop of Water of Sound Doctrine washed the city clean of the defilement and destruction it had suffered. From her privileged place inside Capsule Rom-Eight-Thirty-Three, Josie Faithful looked with amazement on the land below. She and her boss, Miss Candour Communique, had been given a ride with Captain Ready Steadfast in the commander's own Capsule. They now hovered high in the sky above the other Capsules who were flitting hither and thither, dropping their loads of water and returning again and again to refill themselves and cleanse the land.

The Truth newspaper would record the event. It was important for future generations to know. Josie was extremely grateful that Miss Communique had chosen her to be part of the team of observers in the Capsule on this momentous day. She had pads of paper with her, and sharpened pencils, and spare pens of every colour. And, as she watched the scenes unfold below, she scribbled notes about everything she could see.

In The Outskirts of Aletheia the gold crosses were no longer gold.

The gold had all run away under the water, and the wood shrunk and shrivelled too – until there were no gold crosses left at all. The new bridges and crossings over the boundary of Water of Sound Doctrine were completely washed away. They had simply disintegrated under the cleansing water. The camps and fairs and tents and Err Transporters, which had been comfortably entrenched across the Pray-Always Farmlands, were no more. Any shelter made of fabric, wood, plastic, and metal could not withstand the Water of Sound Doctrine. The materials had simply melted and were now running down the sloping fields, washed entirely away. The people quickly followed: scampering and hurrying from the strange, stinging, burning water they could not understand.

Josie took note of the 'Meditation and Dream Interpretation' encampment Timmy specifically requested her to watch for. It was a very large campsite so it was easy to spot. It was covered with a haze which was, Miss Communique informed her, swarms of Sloths. But one big direct hit by a Capsule soon took care of that. Josie wasn't sure what happened to the Sloths – it seemed they dissolved away – but the havoc on the camp was unmistakable. She searched for the purple tent of Ms Wander Palm, of whom Timmy had spoken. But it was no more. There was a large, rather disgusting purple puddle which might have indicated where the tent had been, and the tiny figure of a drenched woman gathering her skirts about her and running down the slopes of the Pray-Always Farmlands and out of Aletheia as if her life depended on it.

One other particularly interesting moment was watching the officials of Err fleeing back to their luxury Err Transporters. They were confused when they reached them, and for a while Josie imagined they were arguing over whether they had found the right Transporter. All the colourful slogans about the Reform Aletheia Competition had been washed away following a direct hit by a low-flying Capsule. Captain Steadfast was heard to comment that he didn't condone the wasteful targeting of vehicles, but he certainly understood the desire to wash the evidence of that awful competition away. The presentation of the prize of one thousand Erona to the winner of the competition was now indefinitely postponed. Josie watched with glee the moment the treasure boxes of Err melted away under the power of the Water of Sound Doctrine, and the gold of Err flew far away across the skies, never to be seen again.

"Ground Rescue, standby." At last the moment had come that Lieutenant Bourne Faithful and his Rescuer troops were waiting for.

"Standing by, sir," replied Bourne, the head of the ground clear-up operation.

Henrietta Wallop tried not to dance on her toes in excitement. She had been allowed to accompany her commanding officer out onto the streets of Aletheia – into the war zone!

"You must do exactly what I say," warned Bourne. "You'll be fetching and carrying and running with messages…"

"Yes, sir, no problem, sir!" Henrietta promised eagerly.

But she was rather dubious about the inclusion of the odd old man known as Dim View in the ground rescue force.

"Is he-should he be, uh, here, sir?" she asked, when she could attract Bourne's attention.

Bourne looked at the strange figure which was Dim View. He was dressed in clothes that didn't fit, and wore glasses which were clearly intended for a man ten times his size. But he was covered in his armour of God[11], and he clutched his Bible in his hand. "He's dressed for the fight," said Bourne, "and he's earned the right through his heroic pursuit of our enemy. Never underestimate the usefulness of a Christian who is ready to fight for the Truth."

"Yes, sir, uh, I mean, no, sir," said Henrietta.

When they reached the streets of the city, Henrietta wasn't quite sure what to expect. A fight at close quarters with their enemies? Ambushes? Skirmishes in the street?

But there was none of that.

There were, in fact, very few invaders left, and those who remained were intent on leaving the city. Henrietta had not observed the battle from the skies; she hadn't seen the cleansing of the entire city by the Water of Sound Doctrine – which was still continuing away from the city centre. But she could see the evidence of what had been done. Incredible though it seemed, the impact of the pure, unadulterated, balanced Water of Sound Doctrine of the Bible sent their enemies fleeing in confusion. The Word of God alone did all that!

The skies were blue overhead; the sun was shining on the damp, clean city streets. Each group of Rescuers went in different directions, dividing up the city and the farmlands and even The Outskirts so that every inch was searched, and surveyed, and cleansed from their enemies. Bourne led his Rescuers to the centre of the city, to Redemption Square itself. The city centre streets they passed through were empty. Now and again a lone Snare or Sloth or Meddler was spied and quickly dispatched by one of Bourne's Rescuers. And at last they reached the cross. The camp of protestors was gone; there was no evidence remaining that they were ever there. Apart from the girl with purple hair who sat quietly on the steps at the foot of the cross.

"Henry," said Bourne quietly. "You can deal with this."

Henrietta wondered what he meant. Should she get rid of her? And yet, if the girl was an enemy of Aletheia, surely she would not have withstood the cleansing effect of the Water of Sound Doctrine.

"Hello," said Henrietta. "I'm Henrietta."

"I'm Crystal," said the girl.

"Did you get left behind?" asked Henrietta.

"I don't know," said Crystal. "I didn't want to go. I met a boy once and he told me to come to the cross. I don't know why the others ran away."

"I think it's because they couldn't stand the Truth," said Henrietta wisely.

"Couldn't they?" said Crystal. "What is the Truth?"

Henrietta sat down beside the girl. "Well, it's all about the Lord Jesus," she began.

And, for a while, that's where Henrietta and Crystal stayed.

The ground forces of Rescuers swept the entire city clean of the creatures of Err. Mr Buffer, assisted by Dusty in the Control Room, kept them informed of the readings on the Rascal Register machine until they were absolutely convinced that none remained. Many had, in any case, left with the people they so closely shadowed; but a few remaining creatures, Meddlers in particular, were dispatched in no uncertain terms.

Dim View patiently followed his leader and stuck with his group until they reached the place he most wanted to see. And when he saw it, he laughed with joy. The tangled hedges and thorn bushes which once surrounded No-Witness Apartments, his old home, were already shrivelled and dying from the Water of Sound Doctrine. The surrounding wall was tumbling down. The apartment block was no longer fit for the purpose of hiding away and not telling anyone about the Lord Jesus. The one remaining resident, who refused to come back to the cross, was standing forlornly at the window, looking terrified and exposed. Then Mr Nil Vision grabbed his packed bag and scurried out of Aletheia to join the folk at the Fearful Christian Commune, not far away. No-Witness Apartments were no more.

That evening, the animals of the Pray-Always farms were released from underground Aletheia. At last Jack and Zek got to see the vast underground ramp – which opened up from the underground and discharged the animals straight onto the farmlands themselves. They were all mixed up and higgledy-piggledy, but the farmers didn't worry about that. What was important was that the farmlands were cleansed, the fields and barns were safe, and the aboveground rivers and streams flowed with the pure, unpolluted Water of Sound Doctrine.

The victory was complete.

CHAPTER 33
THE NEXT STEP

The special edition of *The Truth* newspaper, describing in detail the battle for Aletheia, was highly appreciated by all who read it. Miss Communique was very proud of her star pupil, Josie, who had taken so many accurate notes for the people who wrote the final articles. But it was a challenging report too, and cautioned the people of Aletheia that there was much damage to be repaired and work to be done before the coming of winter. Roads, buildings, bridges, landscaping, planting, ploughing, fencing, salvage – all needed urgent attention.

The weekly edition of the official newspaper of the Council of Err, 'Erra-4-You', was circulated shortly after the battle. It portrayed a very different story of what happened in Aletheia. 'The Aliens of Err' was the title of the article, and the description of the battle caused great indignation amongst the children of Aletheia when they heard of it. The whole debacle was blamed on the *'unhealthy and poisoned'* atmosphere of Aletheia, and the people of Err were warned to stay away. '*A recent toxic rainstorm has rendered the land unsafe,*' said the article. '*The people that remain there are likely to be insane. No attempt should be made to contact them until the official investigation is complete and the atmosphere is declared safe.*'

Chapter 33: The Next Step

The article of lies was no surprise to the managers at the Management Meeting. They were more experienced in the ways of the land of Err. When people refused to accept the Truth, a lie was their only other option. The managers knew the Council of Err would not stop in its efforts to attack and change Aletheia. There would be more to come. And so they met once more to discuss the aftermath of the war, and their plans for the future.

"And now to the matter of the Deceivedor," said the Chief, looking around the table and spotting Dr Theo Pentone, as usual seated by his unlikely friends Philologus Mustardpot and Croft Straw. "Theo?"

Dr Pentone rose with alacrity. "I think we all know the Deceivedor is dead," he said cheerfully. The demise of the Deceivedor was a considerable pleasure to him. He had found the snake in a pile of sticky goo in its dungeon cell one day. He subsequently examined the creature's body with great interest. Dr Pentone had discovered a great deal about Deceivedors – far more than the faraway scientists at the Academy of Science-Explains-All would have thought possible; they would never know how much the clever doctor had uncovered of their creation.

"As we suspected, the Deceivedor was programmed to self-destruct," said Dr Pentone. "However, before the creature's messy demise..." Mr Mustardpot chuckled loudly and showed his own approval by thumping the table. "Before the Deceivedor imploded," continued Dr Pentone, "we did gather enough information to cause us to strongly suspect there is a third and final phase to the Meddlers' – or more accurately the Council of Err's – plan to overthrow Aletheia."

"I always suspected there was a Phase Three," mused the Chief.

"Surely the time has come to go after the Meddlers and stop this nonsense once and for all!" said Mr Mustardpot eagerly. "While the Meddlers are weak and in disarray, let's locate and destroy their headquarters, this Rumour Mill!"

"Which is only rumoured to exist," murmured Captain Steadfast with a smile.

It was hard to believe, now they were once more secure in their city, with all their boundaries clean and intact, that the defeated Meddlers could succeed now. More than likely, the third phase of their plan to defeat Aletheia relied on the success of the second phase – which was a complete disaster as far as the Meddlers and the Council of Err were concerned. Not a single wicked Meddler remained within the city's boundaries: not even in The Outskirts. But the managers knew they must be vigilant; their months underground when their city was invaded had taught them that.

"I suppose none of the children know what this Phase Three might involve?" said Mr Wallop drily. The others smiled. It was, after all, the children who helped to reveal details of both Phase One and Phase Two of the Meddlers' plans for the destruction of Aletheia.

"Perhaps…" said Sturdy Wright slowly, "perhaps it would be worthwhile talking to my son, Benjamin. He did have the most to do with the Deceivedor when the creature was masquerading as Con Cozen. He's got a good memory – perhaps it's worth seeing if Ben can remember something that might help?"

"Sagacia, can I ask you to interview Benjamin Wright?" asked the Chief. "If anyone can help him to remember important information the Deceivedor might have inadvertently dropped, I'm sure you can!"

Sagacia Steady, the Chief Judge of Aletheia, nodded. "Consider it done," she said.

CHAPTER 34
BENJAMIN AND THE JUDGE

The Chief Judge wasted no time in summoning Benjamin Wright for an interview. She arranged for a Junior Justice, Jude Faithful, who was Bourne's younger brother and also a cousin of Benjamin, to collect Benjamin and escort him to her office. Benjamin, who was disappointed that school had recommenced, was delighted to be given special leave by Mr Mustardpot to attend the interview.

"This is great!" he said enthusiastically to his cousin Jude when he reached the grand archways of the Judges' Academy. "Any idea what it's all about?"

Jude was amused. Benjamin was unfailingly cheerful and optimistic. It did not occur to him that anything unpleasant lay ahead. "I'm afraid it's about that business with the Deceivedor, Con Cozen," he said.

"Is it?" said Benjamin, apparently undismayed. "I thought they'd forgotten all about that! They said that since God forgave me because of the Lord Jesus, what I did would be forgiven by them too, and…"

"Oh, they're not going to punish you," Jude said hastily.

"And I apologised to the Rescuer who might have been falsely accused, you know, the one who went through Door Nineteen before I did…"

"Oh, I wouldn't worry about that either," said Jude, leading Benjamin into the Judges' Academy and down a wide, polished corridor.

"And as for Dim View, well, he's a friend now. I visited him only yesterday with a bag of apples – sort of in memory of our time at the Food Distribution Centre."

Jude stifled a chuckle. How the Chief Judge, sober-minded and excessively steady, would manage an interview with Benjamin, he could hardly wait to see. He knocked on the polished dark wood door which displayed 'Chief Judge Steady' in gold lettering upon it, and on her firm, "Come in", ushered Benjamin within.

There were a few quiet moments of nothing while the Judge continued to bend over a document, reading intently. Benjamin took the time to survey her book-lined, thickly carpeted, neat and tidy study.

"Now…" Judge Steady laid down the document she was studying and peered over her small, sparkly glasses at the boy who stood regarding her with frank, unafraid interest. "Benjamin, is it?"

"Yes, ma'am," said Benjamin with a quick grin. "Did you think Jude might have brought the wrong boy?"

The Chief Judge stared at the boy for a heartbeat. Was he being impertinent? But she didn't think so. She had little knowledge of Benjamin Wright, although she was aware he was the best friend of her nephew, Charlie Steady. She didn't think he was a particularly good influence on Charlie; the two boys were known mischief-makers. But Benjamin had an open, honest face, and Mr Mustardpot had assured her that, despite his mischievous streak, his word could be trusted. Besides which, he had recently become a Christian. "Sit down, Benjamin," she said. "You too, Justice Faithful."

"Thanks," said Benjamin. He looked with sudden interest at his cousin, Jude. He had no idea what Jude did all day at the Judges' Academy, but his title sounded kind of grand.

"I want to talk to you about the Deceivedor," said the Judge.

"I know," said Benjamin. "Jude said."

"Well," continued the Judge, "we're hoping you can help us with something important." She spoke slowly and distinctly, as if she was trying to help Benjamin to understand.

Benjamin regarded her doubtfully. For all that she was the Chief Judge, she sounded pretty dim.

"I've been reading about Deceivedors…" She placed her hand on the document she was perusing when they entered.

"Have you?" said Benjamin. "That's funny, because that's exactly what I've been doing too!"

"H-have you?" faltered the Judge.

Jude ducked his head over his notepad, taking copious notes – about nothing at all.

Benjamin nodded solemnly. "I don't want to be deceived again, you see," he said.

"No," said the Judge, "I imagine not."

"Why were *you* reading about them?" asked Benjamin with interest.

Jude kept his head down and wrote faster.

"Because…well, never mind that." The Judge observed the keen, bright glance of Benjamin Wright. Perhaps this boy didn't need help teasing out the details. "To get straight to the point, we believe the Deceivedor, known for a time as Con Cozen, might have known details of another plan for a further attack on Aletheia which hasn't happened yet. Now, he may have said something to you which seemed small and insignificant at the time, which would give us a clue about this. So…"

"You want me to tell you everything he said to me?" asked Benjamin eagerly.

"Exactly," said the Judge.

"Well, that won't be hard," said Benjamin. "Because I'm afraid he didn't say much at all! The only conversation we had was when I... when I unfortunately let him in underground. The times after that," he shrugged. "I'm afraid he was sleeping or ignoring me," he concluded.

"Right," said the Judge briskly. "Well, tell us everything you can about your initial conversation. From what I've read of Deceivedors they really do think they are so clever at deceiving, that they actively enjoy giving hints about the deception, believing no one but them will know what they mean."

"I read that too," said Benjamin. "I think that's why he chose the name, Con Cozen – because it means *deceive*, doesn't it? Only, I didn't realise it at the time."

"Uh, exactly," agreed the Judge, frankly astonished at Benjamin's grasp of the situation. This boy might even make a future Judge! "So, take us through the conversation, and Justice Faithful will record everything."

Justice Faithful was already recording everything. So far it was a very entertaining account.

"Well, first I asked him if he – the old man as he was then – was alright. He was a bit, well, *disagreeable*, to be honest. I remember him saying, 'A-a-alrightss? Iss v-verys w-wets throughs!'" Benjamin was a very good mimic, and the Judge looked incredulous as he gasped like a wheezy, old man with a most realistic hiss and stutter, and a very peculiar accent too. Jude laughed out loud, too amused to even try to cover it.

"It's the way I remember things," explained Benjamin earnestly. "I have to remember how they were said too."

"Very good," said the Judge. She didn't really mind.

"Then I asked him if he was a friend of Aletheia," said Benjamin. "You see, at the time I didn't know the right questions, or about the Truth of the Bible, so I just asked him if he was a friend of Aletheia – which I can see was a bit stupid now. I should have asked him a Bible question, something about the Lord Jesus, but…"

"That's alright," said the Judge hastily. "What did he say?"

"'F-friends? A-Aletheiass?'" Benjamin once more took on the voice of the old man as he quoted him. "Then the old man laughed, and he said, uh…" Benjamin screwed up his face. "He said, 'S-soons there iss no f-friendss!' Yes, I think that was it."

"Stop!" cried the Judge, and Benjamin unscrewed his face with astonishment while Jude almost dropped his pen. "Is that *exactly* what he said?" pressed the Judge eagerly.

"Yes," said Benjamin simply. He had an excellent memory for oddities and unusual things.

"Did you record that exactly, Faithful?" demanded the Judge.

"Yes, ma'am," said Jude.

Benjamin carefully recalled the rest of the conversation, and Jude equally carefully recorded it. But nothing caught the interest of the clever Chief Judge like that single, innocuous statement about friends.

"Did it help?" Benjamin asked, when they had carefully dissected every detail.

"I think, Benjamin," said the Judge, "that you have just revealed the direction of the next planned attack on Aletheia."

Benjamin was very pleased, if somewhat surprised, that he had been able to tell them something important. Who would have thought that that wicked old man – but he must remember he was actually a snake! – would have known anything worth knowing? At last, *at last*, he felt as if he was truly a defender of Aletheia, just like the others were. He was less pleased when the Chief Judge dismissed him kindly but firmly, without divulging any further details. He wished he could know what it all meant.

The door clicked shut, and Jude was left alone with the Judge. He carefully read through the statements that Benjamin had made. Friends. There will be no more friends.

"Do you see it too, Faithful?" asked the Judge quietly.

"Friendship," Jude said thoughtfully. "There will be no more friends. They're going to attack friendship, love, unity…aren't they?"

The Chief Judge removed her glasses and rubbed her tired eyes. "Yes," she agreed.

"How will they do it?" asked Jude.

"I think," the Judge said slowly, "I think they will attack people's character. Through lies, slander, insinuation, stories – oh, they will have endless ways to destroy the credibility of the people of Aletheia! Until we're all at war with each other! And it's my guess they will start at the top."

Jude sat back in his chair. His uncle – Mr Hardy Wallop – he was one of the leaders of Aletheia. The sober Judge sitting on the other side of the desk – she was another. The great, trusted Chief of Aletheia. The heroic Captain Steadfast. The colourful Head of Education, Mr Mustardpot. Kind, hardworking Mr Straw. Peculiar, clever Dr Pentone. Young, pretty, capable Candour Communique. Honourable, likeable Sturdy Wright. They all flashed before him. They were all in danger.

Jude put down his pen. "How can we stop it?" he asked, appalled at the prospect. Even when stories were false, people believed them. This could destroy the leaders of Aletheia; and through that destruction, damage the Truth.

Chief Judge Steady was quiet for a moment. "I think," she said at last, "I think that we must destroy the Rumour Mill."

CHAPTER 35
THE LAST DEFENDER OF ALETHEIA

Jack knew it was time to go home. He must, at last, get back to Harris. As he had made his own way *to* Aletheia, this time he must make his own way *from* Aletheia.

Now all the security measures were relaxed on Underground Entry to Aletheia, Mr Wallop easily arranged his journey on the correct Slide. And, not long after the battle for Aletheia, when his friends were busy helping with the clear up, Jack slipped away. Only Mr Wallop watched him go.

"The others will understand," Jack said bravely. "I always come and go!"

"So you do," said Mr Wallop with a kind smile. "And, when you see him, remember to ask your brother what he's been up to. I have a feeling he's been helping us win the battle too!"

Jack didn't know how that could be and why Mr Wallop thought so. Mr Wallop had never met Harris. But he barely had time to consider the Superintendent's parting words when he was shooting *upwards* at terrifying speed on the wickedly steep Slide, catapulted straight to the opening in the huge cavern which first launched him on his adventure!

Jack noticed there had been a rock fall since he was last there; he had to clamber through big boulders to get into the cavern. He didn't stop to consider what this might mean. He dashed through the cavern to the opening that led up the drainpipe. It was the only opening that hadn't been affected by the rock fall. "Harris!" he called. "Harris! I'm coming!"

He crawled more easily up the pipe than when he came down it; his rucksack felt considerably lighter this time; he had left his *Handbook for Adventurous Boys* and a few other items in Aletheia for Zek. But the pipe was very wet, as if there had recently been a stream running through it. "Harris?" he called again.

A small face peered in the far end of the pipe. "Jack?" It was definitely Harris. And he looked wet too.

Jack crawled out onto the soggy earth floor and looked at his brother in silence. "Was I away for a long time?" he asked at last. There were so many other important things to tell and say, but for a moment he couldn't think of any of them.

Harris shook his head. "I don't think so," he said, "and I was busy keeping guard."

"Guarding what?" asked Jack.

"Snakes," said Harris solemnly.

Jack didn't laugh or disbelieve him. He remembered the awful

Deceivedor which became a humungous snake; he thought about Mr Wallop's parting words – that Harris, too, had played a part in the battle for Aletheia. "Where did the snakes go?" he asked.

Harris was perplexed. "They were here, crowding up the pipe, wanting to get out and go and hurt Aletheia. I blocked them with my Bible and they couldn't get out. But then, just before you came, there was-there was a big flood! It came through the door, across the floor, and went straight down the pipe! And-and it washed them all away! Honestly, you have to believe me…!"

"I do believe you," said Jack. "And wait until you hear the rest of the story!"

They walked the remaining distance home from school. Harris didn't seem to mind he had been left out of a thrilling adventure. He had, after all, been fighting for the good of Aletheia, just like Jack.

He hadn't been idle.

In fact, he was the last defender of Aletheia.

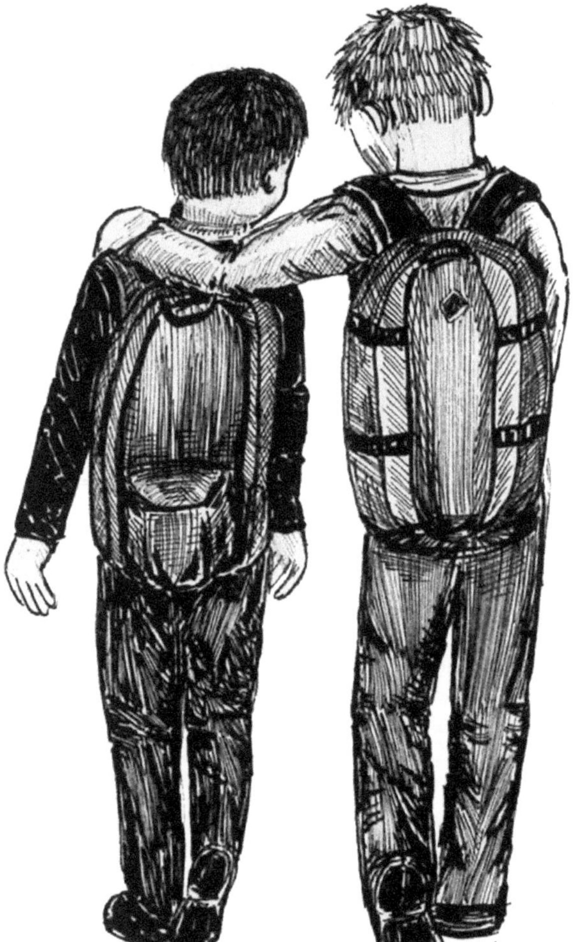
EMW

REFERENCES

Unless otherwise stated, all Bible references are taken from the New King James Version of the Bible.

1. [References on pages 14, 55, 145, 158] The Bible teaches that God has made a way for people to have their sins forgiven and one day go to heaven. People who have trusted in the Lord Jesus are called Christians. There are many verses in the Bible which explain how you become a Christian. For example,

   Acts 16:31:
   "Believe on the Lord Jesus Christ, and you will be saved."

   John 3:16:
   "For God so loved the world that He gave His only begotten Son, that whoever believes in Him should not perish but have everlasting life."

2. [References on pages 18, 101, 119, 123, 124, 249] You can read about this in Book 1 of the Aletheia Adventure Series, The Rescue of Timmy Trial.

3. [References on pages 18, 40, 49, 58, 61, 68, 71, 79, 105, 118, 181]

You can read about this in Book 4 of the Aletheia Adventure Series, The Mustardseeds.

4. [Reference on page 21] There are verses in the Bible which explain that God will answer prayer when we ask something in keeping with His will. (Since the Bible is the Word of God, God's will is always in keeping with the Bible). For example,
John 14:13:
"And whatever you ask in My name, that I will do."

1 John 5:14:
"If we ask anything according to His [God's] will, He hears us."

5. [References on pages 22, 78, 109] You can read about this in Book 3 of the Aletheia Adventure Series, The Broken Journey.

6. [References on pages 30, 100, 111, 160] This is a reference to a verse which explains how the Bible can show us the way.
Psalm 119:105:
"Your word is a lamp to my feet
And a light to my path."

[This doesn't mean that the Bible is a literal light; this verse is saying that the Word of God will be our guide through life if we believe what the Bible says.]

7. [References on pages 40, 106] This is a reference to a verse in the Bible which talks about having faith, even faith as small as a mustard seed.
This verse is found in **Matthew 17:20**:
"So Jesus said to them "...I say to you, if you have faith as a mustard seed...nothing will be impossible for you."

8. [References on pages 44, 51, 100] This is a reference to **Hebrews 4:12**:
"For the word of God is living and powerful, and sharper than any two-edged sword...and is a discerner of the thoughts and intents of the heart."

9. [References on pages 59, 77, 93] The Bible teaches that there is no other way to heaven but through trusting in the Lord Jesus. The Lord Jesus is the mediator – that is, He brings God and people together, and brings people back to God.
This is explained in **1 Timothy 2:5**:

"For there is one God and one Mediator between God and men, the Man Christ Jesus."

[Note that 'men' here means all people.]

The Lord Jesus also said that He was the way back to God. This can be found in **John 14:6**:

"Jesus said to him, "I am the way, the truth, and the life. No one comes to the Father except through Me.""

10. [References on pages 66, 242] You can read about this in Book 2 of the Aletheia Adventure Series, The Purple Storm.

11. [References on pages 72, 73, 76, 84, 98, 107, 109, 118, 164, 254] The Bible talks about Christians putting on the 'armour of God'. This is explained in **Ephesians 6:10-18**:

"Finally, my brethren, be strong in the Lord and in the power of His might.

Put on the whole armour of God, that you may be able to stand against the wiles of the devil. For we do not wrestle against flesh and blood, but against principalities, against powers, against the rulers of the darkness of this age, against spiritual hosts of wickedness in the heavenly places. Therefore take up the whole armour of God, that you may be able to withstand in the evil day, and having done all, to stand.

Stand therefore, having girded your waist with truth, having put on the breastplate of righteousness, and having shod your feet with the preparation of the gospel of peace; above all, taking the shield of faith with which you will be able to quench all the fiery darts of the wicked one. And take the helmet of salvation, and the sword of the Spirit, which is the word of God; praying always with all prayer and supplication in the Spirit…"

12. [References on pages 77, 92, 124, 127, 217] The cross represents the death of the Lord Jesus. There are verses in the Bible which describe how He died on a cross to save people from their sins. For example,

    Romans 5:8:
    "God demonstrates His own love toward us, in that while we were still sinners, Christ died for us."

    Philippians 2:5-8:
    "Christ Jesus…coming in the likeness of men…He humbled Himself and became obedient to the point of death, even the death of the cross."

13. [References on pages 96, 125] Money growing wings and flying away is a reference to

Proverbs 23:5:

"Will you set your eyes on that which is not?
For riches certainly make themselves wings;
They fly away like an eagle toward heaven."

[The Bible does not mean that money literally flies; this verse is saying that riches are easily lost.]

14. [References on pages 102, 143, 226] The Bible talks about the truth of 'justification'. God can justify someone because of the sacrifice of the Lord Jesus when He died on the cross, so that anyone who trusts in Him can have their sins forgiven. To 'justify' simply means God can make someone completely right again – just as if they'd never sinned. If someone trusts in the Lord Jesus, all their sins are blotted out and they are ready to go to heaven. A verse about justification is **Romans 3:23-24**:
"For all have sinned and fall short of the glory of God, being justified freely by His grace through the redemption that is in Christ Jesus."

15. [References on pages 124, 224, 226] 'Sin' is the Bible name for all the wrong things that everyone has done. The Bible teaches that everyone has sinned against God and doesn't meet His standards. There is a verse about this in **Romans 3:23**:
"For all have sinned and fall short of the glory of God."

16. [References on pages 139, 145] Benjamin thinks the Bible doesn't work for him because his Bible doesn't show light. This illustrates that someone must believe in the truth of the Bible – then the Bible becomes light to them: they are able to understand and do what the Bible says.

17. [Reference on page 225] This verse is found in **Romans 3:26**:
"To demonstrate at the present time His righteousness, that He might be just and the justifier of the one who has faith in Jesus."

18. [Reference on page 237] The Bible teaches that once we have trusted in the Lord Jesus, our sins are forgiven and completely blotted out. This means, as far as God is concerned, they don't exist anymore.
Psalm 103:12:
"As far as the east is from the west,

So far has He removed our transgressions from us."

Acts 3:19:

"Repent therefore and be converted, that your sins may be blotted out."